2-50

The Rise and Fall of Freddie Laker

The Rise and Fall of Freddie Laker

HOWARD BANKS

faber and faber

First published in 1982
by Faber and Faber Limited
3 Queen Square London WC1N 3AU
Printed in Great Britain by
Redwood Burn Ltd., Trowbridge, Wiltshire
All rights reserved

© *Howard Banks, 1982*

British Library Cataloguing in Publication Data

Banks, Howard
  The rise and fall of Freddie Laker.
  1. Laker, *Sir* Freddie   2. Aeronautics—
  Great Britain—Biography   3. Aeronautics,
  Commercial—Great Britain—History
  4. Businessmen—Great Britain—Biography
  I. Title
  387.7'42'0924   HE9911
  ISBN 0–571–11986–7
  ISBN 0–571–13077–1 (Pbk)

Contents

Acknowledgements

Many people in the aviation business gave freely of their time to help me prepare this book. Many of them prefer to remain anonymous. I thank them all. Special thanks go to former colleagues at the *Economist*, particularly those in the Library.

Without the help, guidance and encouragement of Joan Feldman, aviation journalist-extraordinary (and my wife), it would not have been possible to write this book at all, let alone in so short a time.

H.B.

Prologue: The lionization of Laker

Right up until the last minute, Sir Freddie Laker maintained that all was going to turn out satisfactorily. His airline was not going to go broke; the bankers were going to rescue him. During the final days of efforts to create a financial package that would save the company, he had even announced prematurely that such a package had been arranged, angering the bankers who were still trying. It was an act of foolish outspokenness that helped to push Laker Airways over the edge. At the end, Laker was still telephoning and holding meetings up to midnight on Thursday, 4 February 1982, but could find no one, friend or rival, who would buy parts of his business to provide the money to keep the rest alive. At 8 a.m. the following morning, the receivers were called in.

Immediately there was an outpouring of public sympathy for this intensely likable man. The telephones at Laker Airways' headquarters at Gatwick Airport buzzed with offers of help and promises of donations. In all, it was later said, there was around £3½ million on offer through a Save Sir Freddie Laker fund, set up with the help of Lloyds Bank.

The size of the fund was unprecedented—far larger than for many natural disasters. The public were not dissuaded by evidence, widely reported in newspapers and on radio and television, that the airline had been badly mismanaged financially and that Laker was, to a large extent, responsible for his own downfall. The mythology that had grown up around Laker was stronger than any amount of proof of his own weaknesses. This overwhelming reaction of the British public to the collapse was partly the result of the country's depressed economy and its attendant lack of morale. Britain needed heroes, and Laker fitted the bill.

The reasons are all genuine and easily understood. Laker's story is the classic one of a factory tea-boy who, through hard work and effort, turned himself into a jet-setting millionaire. To achieve fame and fortune, he had to take on both the British and American Governments, and the International Air Transport Association (IATA), the international airlines' cartel. He appealed to the courts, as a man of the common people, and justice came down firmly on his side. For a while, after his successful battle in the courts led to the inauguration of his Skytrain service in 1977, he was hardly ever out of the newspapers or off the television screens. He was St Fred, hero of air travellers, one of 'us'; he was the man who was seen to have introduced cheap air travel that ordinary people could afford. Admittedly it was only across the North Atlantic, but soon it would spread to all routes—wouldn't it? All this warrior had to do was to take on those representatives of the establishment ('Them') several more times.

At 6 ft 1 in tall, Laker is a larger-than-life character. His chubby face is usually blessed with a wide grin, which obviously lapsed a little at the end when his dreams were collapsing around him. He has always retained his Kentish accent from his birthplace in Canterbury, and has never curbed his outspoken and sometimes vulgar manner of speaking. He has described civil servants as 'bums and gangsters' and stirred echoes in every other Briton's heart. There has never been any pretension or artificial snobbery about Laker. He has enjoyed being a success and a well-known public figure. The limelight suits him; he makes no secret of it, and the public—mainly in Britain, but also in Australia and the United States—has always warmed to him. He was even approached at one time about becoming a politician to publicize the virtues of the free enterprise system. While he confessed he had thought about it, his abrasive views about politicians would have made such a career change difficult.

This entrepreneur adopted the trappings of wealth with a will, and nobody resented it. He has always had an eye for pretty ladies and large, luxurious cars. In 1953 he was driving an Austin Princess, a very large car by the British standards of the time. But it was too much when his opposite number at British Eagle, Harold Bamberg, who was his most serious rival among British independent airline operators, turned up at Laker's office in a Bentley. So Laker went out and purchased the first of twenty-six

Rolls-Royces. He is also partial to special number plates for his cars. His own is FAL 1, after his initials. He was given FLY 1 by the family of the late Lord Brabazon of Tara, the first British airman to hold a pilot's licence. Now, after the collapse, he is reduced to the Mini Metro that was a present from Airbus Industrie when it delivered the first of his Airbus A300s.

As he became wealthier, Laker steadily moved to grander houses, ending up with a large Tudor home at Chailey, near Lewes in East Sussex. Complete with peacocks in the grounds, it was put on the market just before the collapse for £350,000. Also up for grabs after the collapse were his 1,000 acre Woolgars Farm at West Horsley, Surrey, which was valued at £1 million, and a stud farm at Woodcote Park near Epsom. Perhaps his favourite toy was a large motor yacht that he kept at Palma, Majorca. The yacht was actually owned by Laker Airways and the receiver fell foul of the Spanish authorities when he tried to recover it. Laker used to hold riotous parties well into the small hours on the 85-ton *Tutinella*, which was replaced two years ago by the £600,000 *Patrina*, named after his now-estranged third wife, Patricia, and stepdaughter, Bettina.

But for all this, Laker has always been just as happy having beer and sandwiches in a pub as going to a smart restaurant for lunch. He switches from champagne to a pint of beer with little concern. When he was at home at Chailey he would drop in to his local pub, the Five Bells, for a drink and a chat. He has always taken a genuine interest in people's experiences with air travel, especially when they had travelled on his airline, and he has acted on what they have told him.

Laker enjoyed his image of being Sir Galahad rushing to the aid of the travelling public, the man who rescued ordinary people (he christened them the 'forgotten people') from the established airlines and the governments that backed them. He came to believe that he was invincible, especially after the famous court victory over the British Government in 1977. 'I never really set off to get into a fight. But somehow the fun always starts in situations where there are the greatest opportunities.' On the first Skytrain flight from Gatwick to New York on 26 September 1977, he hugged one of his close aides, Robin Flood, and said to her: 'Well, what are we going to fight for now?'

His fighting for the impossible, in the shape of routes to

Australia, Hong Kong and then on round the world with what he called Globetrain, and the expansion of his fleet of aircraft in advance of getting those routes, got him into trouble. In the end it killed his business. At different stages during this overexpansion, Laker Airways' existence became useful to first the British, then the American Governments and then the British again. The politicians made use of Laker when it suited them to do so, and played a part in his downfall.

There is a wide gulf between the public's perception of Frederick Alfred Laker, Knight Bachelor, and the truth about the collapse of his airline. The world's airlines had lost their shirts in the period of Laker Airways' bankruptcy. Those carriers on the North Atlantic alone lost $600 million in 1981. Just three months after Laker went broke, so did Braniff International in the United States. It, too, succumbed as a result of deregulation, not because there is anything wrong in increasing competition among the airlines—far from it—but because Braniff, like Laker Airways, had overexpanded and overreached itself before the market could recover in time to save it.

How Laker got into this situation is a complex story. It involves not just the man and his ambitions, fed by an excess of flattery from an admiring world, but also the aviation policies of the British and American Governments. As they developed and interacted between 1966, when Laker Airways was set up, and 1982, when it died, so they swept Laker along. Many of these political developments had nothing specific to do with Laker or his operation; he was carried along by currents that at times he seemed not to comprehend and that he rarely controlled. That the public's view of Laker and his role remained otherwise to the end explains why he has been so useful politically.

1 · Self-made man

Laker grew up in a typical working-class home—two up, two down, with an outside lavatory and no bathroom. In 1927, his merchant seaman father deserted his mother—an event that scarred young Freddie, who was only 5. He still resents what his real father did, though the memory of his stepfather helps. His mother remarried when he was 8 and his stepfather (whom Laker called 'Dear') changed his name by deed-poll to Laker, to match his ready-made family.

Laker's mother, to whom he became very close, ran a scrapyard for a time, then a general store that sold almost everything, from toothpaste and stationery to vegetables and clothes. Laker learned well the lesson of how to make an honest penny by hard work. He was not the best scholar—in fact, he wasted most of his time at school—but he ran the school tuck shop. And though he did not make any money directly from this, he got free tuck.

His interest in aircraft was aroused by seeing the *Hindenburg* airship, in the same patch of sky as an Imperial Airways biplane, over Canterbury in 1936. On leaving school, he rode his bike over to Short Brothers in Rochester, an aircraft company that built seaplanes, and asked for a job. His poor school record didn't help, but he was given an apprenticeship of sorts, making tea and sweeping the floors. His ability to turn opportunity into profit soon showed. To avoid being shouted at for spilling quantities of tea on the way back from the canteen, Laker purchased the tea in bulk and poured it into the men's cans in the workshop. He charged the same penny-a-can price, but negotiated a bulk rate for the tea with the canteen lady.

Short's was bombed in 1940 and soon after Laker joined the Air

Transport Auxiliary where he worked as an engineer and ferry
pilot.

He obviously had a way with the ladies from the start. He had
met his first wife, Joan, at a dance when he was just 17. She was six
years his senior. He told a few white lies about his age and they
were married two years later, in 1942. In 1944 their daughter,
Elaine, was born.

After the war, he tried British European Airways for a short
while, but didn't take to corporate life as an engineer. So he began
trading on his own account. He bought surplus army lorries two at a
time for £10–20 each, fixed them up and then resold them, often for
more than £100 apiece. He bought and sold surplus spare parts for
aircraft from a lock-up garage in Streatham. Twice he tried
horticulture. The first time, with £25 of his own money and the rest
borrowed from friends and relations, he paid £250 for the crop
from a cherry orchard that was still in blossom. That was only a
modest financial success. Next he toured east Kent in an old Ford
van and sold seedlings to housewives. As a town boy, he had little
idea how to tell a lettuce seedling from a cabbage seedling. So he
stuck the leaves of the different plants on a crib sheet hidden on the
inside of the van's door.

The tide turned for Laker when he got into the aviation business
in a big enough way to cash in on the Berlin airlift of 1948–9. He
had once taken a job with a company owned by a man called Bobby
Sanderson. Sanderson was unaware that his company was on the
point of going broke, but Laker informed him that it was and
advised him to get his money out while he could. Later Sanderson
repaid the favour and lent Laker £38,000 so that he could buy his
first batch of aircraft, which he used to make more than 4,000 runs
during the Berlin airlift. By this time, Laker had turned his £40
gratuity from the ATA into around £4,000 with his spares company
in Streatham, called Aviation Traders. It was this same company,
together with another, Air Charter, that he sold in 1958—during
the formation of what was to become British United Airways— for
£800,000.

Once, when asked at school what he wanted to be when he grew
up, Laker replied that he 'wanted to be a millionaire'. Given his
circumstances, all that raised was a laugh. Later, when he was at
the top of the heap at Laker Airways, he said: 'I don't want to be a
multi-millionaire. I just want to get by.' In the end, that did not

work out. On another occasion, however, he also confessed that he would not like to be poor again.

2 · The build-up of Laker Airways

Laker is a one-man band; he did his best when he was his own boss. He didn't like working at British European Airways (BEA) immediately after the war, where he was just one of a teeming army of engineers. Even though he was managing director of British United Airways (BUA), which was formed from the merger of a number of companies (including Laker's), he was clearly not the boss. That role was reserved for its chairman, the late Sir Myles Wyatt. He was as urbane as Laker can be blunt, but he knew his way round the business world and taught the entrepreneurial Laker a lot, especially about raising finance in the City. But Wyatt kept a close eye on what was going on and this rankled with Laker, who was used to making up his mind as he went along.

Laker had been thinking of leaving BUA for some time, and setting up on his own once again. Following the sale of his companies in 1958 to the group that became BUA, he was, by the standards of the time, independently wealthy. He dreamed of having an airline of his own and a travel company to run. Laker announced his resignation, due to take effect at the end of the year. In the event, he left in a huff in November of that year, officially over some unspecified policy dispute with Wyatt.

And so, at the age of 43, Laker launched his own airline. At a press conference in February 1966, he said it was to be a low-cost operation dealing only with the inclusive holiday tour operators. At this stage there was no intention in Laker's mind of operating scheduled services.

The company, Laker Airways, was set up in a tax haven, Jersey, which also meant that Britain's restrictive labour laws could be avoided. In effect, these laws allow the unions to demand the same wages from the small, independent airlines as they get from the state-owned carriers. Laker was determined to get round such restrictions as he had fallen out with the trade unions in a big way at BUA. The new airline had just £10,000 of fully paid-up capital, 90 per cent of it in Laker's own name and 10 per cent in the hands of Joan, his first wife. Despite Laker's subsequent remarriages, Joan held that stake right up to the airline's collapse. A parallel company, Laker Leasing, was set up in Britain with the same share split, in order to obtain the operator's licence needed to run a British-based airline.

At the time, Laker said he believed that the 'inclusive tour holiday trade is about to explode' and, in general terms, he was right. However, it turned out that he had picked a tough year to start up. Laker claimed to be creating the first specialist airline company to operate exclusively in the package tour industry. Typically, he had also dreamed up a new way to cash in on that market, called time charters. The idea was to contract with a package tour operator for the exclusive use of an aircraft for the year, a 'personalized airline' he called it. Laker's name was to appear in modestly small letters on the tail of the aircraft, but the tour operator's name would be emblazoned on the side, almost as though the tour company was the owner. Laker's only self-indulgence was to paint the aircraft in the bold red and black stripes that were his horse-racing colours.

Confidence exuded from him as he also announced that he had ordered from the British Aircraft Corporation three BAC 1-11s for around £4 million. The rest of the industry was not clear how he had managed to finance such a deal, but he had put up £211,500 of his own money and borrowed most of the rest from the Clydesdale Bank, now a subsidiary of the Midland Bank and a major lender involved with his airline right up to the bankruptcy. The money-raising lessons from Sir Myles Wyatt had paid off.

BAC helped by underwriting some of the loan, which is a fairly common practice nowadays, but was much less usual then. In part, this was a repayment of an old debt of gratitude by BAC: Laker had been instrumental in launching the BAC 1-11 when he was head of British United Airways. The state-run airline, BEA (later the short-haul part of British Airways), had decided to buy the

Trident from Hawker Siddeley. Laker took on the BAC 1-11 as a pet project, encouraging its designers and allowing them the freedom to match the design to the needs of the airlines in the United States, the largest market for such an aircraft. As a result the BAC 1-11 was, by European standards, a success, selling 230 over twenty years or so (though this was not enough to cover the project's initial development cost and to pay a reasonable return as well).

Time charters were planned to put a minimum of 1,700 and a maximum of 2,300 flying hours a year on each of the BAC 1-11s, the most he could manage without having to hire extra flight crews. For the first 1,700 hours, the operator with exclusive use would pay around £300 an hour, with penalties built into the contract if all the hours were not used. Between that figure and the maximum allowed, the rate per hour would be cut to around £200. The tour operator also had to agree to some fairly tough conditions, such as guaranteeing a fifty-minute turnround for the aircraft at each end of its run. The time booked for each flight was calculated to the minute, from the time the aircraft left the ramp until it came to a halt at its destination.

It all sounded so simple. The tour operators were to do all the selling, leaving Laker to look after flying the aircraft. While the new airline was to do all its own day-to-day maintenance, it had even contracted out major overhauls to Air Couriers, which was also based at Gatwick. In return for having a commitment for a year from the tour operator, Laker was to provide a period free of problems over the availability of an aircraft to carry the tour company's customers.

Translated by the larger, more conservative companies in the tour business, that formula also sounded like a large risk: what if they could not fill the aircraft? For that reason, Laker was unable to sell the idea to the major companies that he had hoped would set the seal on his venture. Thomas Cook, then owned by British Rail, wouldn't budge, despite Laker's persuasive arguments. So he had to make do with two smaller operators, Wings (a commercial operation that had its roots in the Youth Hostelling Association) and Lord Brothers (where Laker had connections from his BUA days). In the end, the Wings contract began on 24 March 1967 and the Lord Brothers deal one day later.

The gap between the formation of Laker Airways, the hiring of a staff of only 120, and the arrival of his first BAC 1-11 in December 1966 was filled in two ways. He arranged a deal to use BAC's own demonstrator 1-11 for training during the autumn, and he bought two Britannia four-engined turboprop airliners from British Overseas Airways Corporation (BOAC—later the long-haul part of British Airways). These Britannias were surplus to BOAC's requirements, since they had been overtaken by the faster, and hence more productive, Boeing 707 jet airliners that the airline had ordered for its North Atlantic routes. With his usual eye for a bargain, Laker got them cheap, at £375,000. Conveniently, many of his newly hired but otherwise unemployed flight crews and staff (many of them ex-BUA) were trained on Britannias.

Once he had taken delivery of the two Britannias, in May and July of 1966, Laker put them to work on charters, getting business where he could. Almost 10,000 passengers were carried this way by the end of the year, putting some cash into the company's till where little had been expected. The new airline declared a profit of £39,000 in its first year of operation. The Britannias were also used in the mini airlift that was mounted to help supply Zambia with oil following Britain's imposition of economic sanctions late in 1965 against Ian Smith's UDI in Rhodesia. This embargo hurt Zambia in particular, since it cut that country's rail link through land-locked Rhodesia to Mozambique's ports. This connection also led to a deal that satisfactorily occupied Laker's third BAC 1-11 when it was proving hard to find an additional company in Britain willing to sign up and join Wings and Lord Brothers. This third BAC 1-11 was painted in Air Congo's colours and flown as part of that airline by Laker's crews and maintenance people.

While his airline flourished, Laker was not without domestic problems. After nearly twenty-five years of marriage, he was divorced by Joan and promptly married Rosemary Black, a South African.

Not being able to find a taker for the third 1-11 was a pointer to the sagging fortunes of the package holiday business in Britain in 1967. There had been an Arab–Israeli war, a coup in Greece and one of Britain's perennial economic crises. This had led to a 14·7 per cent devaluation of the pound sterling and the imposition of a £50 limit on the amount of currency a Briton could take out of the country for a holiday. The 30 per cent annual growth in the number of people taking package holidays from Britain that had occurred during the previous three years dropped to a growth of only 12 per cent in 1967 over the year before. This resulted in a price war among the tour operators to get holiday-makers at any price; margins were slashed to a profit of just £1 per head per tour. When the load factor (the percentage of seats filled) dropped below the 90 per cent or so that the tour business reckoned to be its target for break-even, hefty losses became the rule.

Like a ripple spreading on a pond, first one of the smaller tour companies went to the wall and then others. In one deal, Laker had contracted to carry tourists for Arrowsmith, one of the earliest companies in the package tour business. Arrowsmith was one member of a consortium of tour companies that rapidly began to fall apart in 1967. When its founder, Harry Smith, went into hospital for a heart operation, Laker took the rest of the industry by complete surprise and bought the company. He claimed the price was £500,000, though it was nearer to two-thirds that sum.

Going completely against what he had said when launching Laker Airways, and what he had maintained in the meantime, Laker reversed his policy about sticking to running an airline and leaving the holiday business to others. Buying Arrowsmith, he intoned, was part of his policy of vertical integration, which was 'vitally important' to stabilize and perhaps even cut the cost of package holidays. In these hard-pressed times, cutting the price of a holiday was actually the last thing that anybody else in the business was thinking about. But integrating the tour business with the airline that carried the passengers offered one way to cut costs; it was just what Laker had originally had in mind.

Time charters, for which Laker received an award from the *Daily Telegraph* as the greatest contribution to the travel industry, did not make the two tour operators as much money as they expected. But Lord Brothers, relying on wildly optimistic forecasts derived from their computer, said that they wanted a second BAC 1-11 for 1968. On trust, Laker ordered one for delivery early in that year, plus a fifth to arrive soon after. His expansion plans mounted. A deal with the British Airports Authority made Laker Airways a major operator from Britain's second (and always second-class) airport at Gatwick, where he built a large jet base and some low-cost administrative headquarters. He talked about buying all sorts of aircraft, from a much used VC-10 from BAC, to all the types that companies dream about on their drawing boards, eventually to two

Boeing 707s, which he acquired in 1969 to replace his very tired Britannias.

Somehow, Laker seemed to be able to keep his head above water. In 1968, it soon became apparent that Lord Brothers' belief in their computer forecasts had undone them; the tour company could expect barely enough business to fill one BAC 1-11, let alone the second one Laker had ordered on their behalf. Laker was owed what he claimed was £500,000 by Lord Brothers. As that company began to sink, he pounced. Now he owned two tour operators.

One of the reasons that Laker seemed able to buck the tide was that he had integrated his activities and so was able to control his own costs, especially the time and money that was wasted when aircraft were idle. There was plenty of growth in charter travel from Britain during this period. In 1955, a total of 2 million Britons holidayed abroad, with around a quarter of them travelling on charter flights. By 1972, some 8·5 million Britons holidayed abroad, with around 60 per cent going by charter carriers. Laker had also gone all out to offer discount winter holidays; and to encourage tour operators to do the same, to fill what was otherwise dead time. In what the *Economist* later described as the 'holiday roller coaster', there were barely 20,000 package tourists a month from Britain in the winter of 1968, against about 300,000 a month in the summer peak period. By 1972, thanks to price cutting—and those tantalizing winter breaks of three or four days for under £15 that first wooed the British to rush for sun out of season—the difference had been sharply reduced. That winter, there were more than 200,000 package tourists a month from Britain, compared with 500,000 or so in summer.

For the sharper companies in the tour business, winter profits— aided by being able to contract for low-cost, out-of-season hotel space—were sufficient to offset the summer losses caused by suicidal price cutting. As the tour business had grown and developed, so had the British Government removed the price controls that had once prevented any tour being sold for less than the cheapest scheduled air fare to that destination. The weaker tour companies could not stand the competitive pressure and the pattern of tour companies collapsing, usually at the height of the season, continued. British Eagle, owned by Laker's contemporary, Harold Bamberg, went under at the end of 1968. Clarkson Holidays collapsed in 1973 and was acquired by Court Line, which had been flying its customers. And finally there was the infamous bankruptcy of Court Line itself in 1974.

It is tempting to draw close parallels between the demise of Court Line and Laker's own collapse. Court Line had grown at a far more rapid pace than its management, which had come from the shipping industry, had foreseen. The company had a five-year contract to carry Clarkson's passengers and had acquired two Lockheed TriStars. The deal for these aircraft looked good, but they proved to be too large for the European package tour business of the time and, with only two in the fleet, appallingly expensive to maintain. When Clarkson went broke, Court Line had a choice: either to go broke too, or to take over its key customer, which had been providing 50 per cent of its business. Clarkson's business was as unprofitable for Court Line as it had been for Clarkson, even though the transfer price was, according to rumour at the time, just £1 for an 85 per cent stake.

With another cut-price charter operator, Airfair, and a villa holiday company, OSL, already in its group, Court Line found the going impossible. This was the period just after the Yom Kippur war between Israel and Egypt, OPEC's quadrupling of crude oil prices and its embargo on oil supplies to the West. The travel industry as a whole had turned a collective profit of around £1 million a year in 1969 into a collective loss of £8 million in 1971, £6 million in 1972 and £9 million in 1973.

Court Line should never have survived into 1974, but the unhappiness that would have followed the collapse of a company that accounted for about one-third of the holiday business was the last thing that the Wilson Government wanted. Following the inconclusive result of the general election of February 1974, Edward Heath had resigned and the Labour Government had come into power with no overall majority. Wilson planned to go to the country again within a short time to try to gain a majority in Parliament (which turned out to be in October 1974). So, in order to prevent Court Line's collapse, the Government purchased Court Line's shipbuilding business for £16 million. This strategy failed, because the £16 million turned out to be inadequate to see the tour operator even through the peak summer travel season. To have succeeded, the original plan would have required a bail-out of nearer £25 million. Court Line died because of its excessive ambition and overexpansion in the face of a price war in a near-stagnant market, and at a time when it had insufficient financial reserves to cope.

The circumstances were different, but the eventual verdict on Laker's collapse is remarkably similar. Back in 1968–9, however, Laker had more immediate concerns, ones that were outside the European package tour business that he had come to know well. A major change was evident on the North Atlantic market and had been for some time. The charter segment of the total traffic was beginning to grow rapidly. During the period 1963–7 a fairly steady 15–16 per cent of passengers travelling by air across the Atlantic used charter carriers (or supplementals, as the Americans call them). The share taken by charters began to increase in 1968, when it reached 19 per cent, and by 1969 it was no less than 26·2 per cent. The peak year for charters turned out to be 1971, with almost 30 per cent.

Laker wanted a share of this market and his chance came in 1969, after British Eagle went bust. He put in a bid for the two Boeing 707s that Eagle had recently acquired from the Australian flag carrier, Qantas—an airline with a deserved reputation for looking after its equipment. Laker leased them from the receiver, which avoided the necessity to find the fairly large cash sum that would have been needed to buy them outright.

Running charters on the North Atlantic was complicated by a set of rules that can only be described as Byzantine. They arose out of a decision made in 1953 by the international airlines' cartel, the International Air Transport Association (IATA). Since some of its strongest members, such as Pan American and BOAC, wanted to run a few such charters—and in time they became the largest charter carriers on the North Atlantic—the cartel decided to let them. It had little choice if it was to stay together. But the rest of the members imposed such rigid rules and conditions as to make operating charters next to impossible, or so it was thought. Low-fare charters could be set up only where there was a pre-existing group with what was described as 'sufficient affinity', though what was sufficient was defined merely as six months' membership of a group before the date of departure. The nature of the group had clearly to set it aside from the general public—for example, rose growers, Scots who had emigrated, even government department staff associations. No group could have more than 20,000 members, to cut out useful clubs such as motoring associations.

And to make it even less likely that such charters could be arranged, the travel agents were to be limited to a 5 per cent commission.

A turning point for these charters on the North Atlantic came in 1963, when Caledonian (years before it had acquired BUA to form British Caledonian) persuaded the American Civil Aeronautics Board (CAB) to set aside the objections of scheduled airlines like Pan Am and BOAC, and grant it a three-year blanket permit to fly charters from the United States to Britain. The permit was signed by President John F. Kennedy in the summer of that year. This case fits in with a continuing contrast between the aviation policies of Democratic and Republican administrations in Washington. Democrats favour the consumer and increased competition between the air carriers, while the Republicans favour what big business (in this case the major airlines) wants for a quiet life. This Kennedy decision on charters gave the British regulatory body, at that time the Air Transport Licensing Board, a problem, since it did not much like the idea of these low-cost charters. By the time Laker's turn came to apply for the necessary permits and licences, it was more or less a routine matter, providing it was conducted in the correct manner. For Washington, that meant finding an American lawyer who knew what to do, and here—once again—Laker fell on his feet. He chose Bob Beckman, who is still his lawyer and who, even after Laker Airways' bankruptcy twelve years later, is still fighting for his client. For years, Beckman stalked the halls of the CAB, the State Department and politicians' offices on Capitol Hill. For all his skill in dealing with aviation law, Beckman has a knack of being able to rub people up the wrong way just passing the time of day. Nonetheless, it was Beckman who, in the meantime, helped Laker beat the whole weight of the British Government in the British courts.

By the time Laker Airways entered the North Atlantic charter market, the fiddles were rife over who was, and who was not, a member of six months' standing in some group or other. It took no ingenuity whatsoever for passengers to find a travel agent, especially in London, who would backdate a membership form. When the difference was travelling for about £40 one-way compared with a normal scheduled economy return fare of at least £240, what else did the regulators expect?

Nevertheless, efforts were made to police what was going on

and, not surprisingly, as the latest carrier in the market, Laker was the most vulnerable to such fiddles. Typically, he adopted a stance that looked good but was not terribly practical. He made all his passengers sign an affidavit, either separately or as part of their tickets. People are basically honest, Laker pronounced, but they were obviously not quite so honest when it came to getting cheap travel. Steedman Hinckley, the head of the American charter carrier Overseas National, was less squeamish about charter fiddles. He told a Senate hearing:

> I would go so far as to say that I think that there are members of the clergy, or congregations of churches, who without the slightest feeling of guilt would sign [that they had been members of some group for six months] because they know they are being cheated by the CAB, which is trying to keep American citizens off low-cost transportation when there is no justification for doing so.

Other charter operators, including Caledonian, were caught out by spot checks, but the worst cases seemed to plague Laker Airways. The most notorious example occurred in May 1971, when about a quarter of the passengers booked as part of an American group called the Left Hand Club, were found by a spot check not to be bona fide members. They were taken off the aircraft. The whole sordid episode, complete with weeping grandmothers who had spent all their holiday cash, was filmed by Britain's Independent Television News. It had been tipped off, but by whom is the subject only of libellous rumour. The row that followed ended the raids, but the problem of false club memberships had by that time gone too far to be halted.

Laker was in even more trouble in the United States with the CAB, which had a list of over 200 of Laker's charters that had broken the rules. And the Board had first-hand proof: some CAB employees had replied to advertisements, which by then were commonplace in most major newspapers, and had travelled 'illegally' on Laker's charter flights. Laker was also upsetting the American authorities by refusing to supply them with the volume of information that they thought they were entitled to receive about his business. The Americans have habitually collected masses of data about civil aviation, some of it useless, but they do not expect to be refused whatever they ask for. In part this explains the sour relationship that existed for years between the American authorities and Laker.

The effect of all this surveillance on Laker Airways was drastic. According to Laker's own testimony to the British Civil Aviation Authority, his carrier had flown around 150 charters between the United States and Britain in 1970. With the combined weight of the CAA and the CAB on its back, the total in 1971 was down to just twelve flights—a reduction that had nothing to do with any decline in demand.

It was in the immediate aftermath of the televised raid at Gatwick that Laker formalized the idea that emerged at the end of June 1971 as Skytrain. The idea had been floating around at the back of his mind for years. He had said to colleagues when still at BUA, as he watched people checking in at London's Victoria Station to catch a train to Gatwick, that what aviation needed was something equally simple. He had, in fact, registered the name Skytrain during 1970. Such a scheme might now solve the rows over affinity groups by allowing people what they obviously wanted: an instant-booking, low-fare means of travelling between the United States and Britain. And no doubt, he thought and planned, to many other places as well.

There were easier charter rules already in force on routes from Britain to the Far East and to India. And BOAC, always a little more adventurous than most people gave it credit for, had managed to institute its advance purchase fares—called Earlybird—on its scheduled services to Bermuda. For all sorts of protectionist reasons, the Americans at this time simply would not hear of allowing this type of fare on scheduled routes to the United States. And the American authorities, together with the British, wouldn't hear of Skytrain either. It was the beginning of a six-year saga for Laker.

3 · An eye for opportunity

Laker's skill has often resided in finding a hole in a market that somebody is not filling or is filling inadequately. He has not always been first in the way that he was with time charters and with the Skytrain concept, but he has often worked out how to do things in a more marketable way. In 1951, when he first began operating his own aircraft as an airline operator, he was very much the johnny-come-lately into the government troop-carrying business. The War Office had calculated that flying troops was cheaper, and quicker, than sending them by ship to Britain's still extensive and far-flung military bases. The Royal Air Force did not have the aircraft (or the money to buy them) to take on this work. It was argued that this trade would support independent airlines in case they were needed. The Americans used much the same argument in later years to justify protecting their independent charter, or supplemental, operators.

Air troop-carrying grew rapidly and, in the early 1950s, was dominated by four independent carriers: Skyways, Airwork, Hunting and Eagle. Most of the flying was done in almost worn-out wartime aircraft, such as converted bombers or York transports. To break into this market Laker improved the quality of the Yorks he proposed to use. They were, for example, clean and had usable lavatories. They were also maintained in better condition than usual and fitted with better seats. These faced rearwards, for safety reasons, and had headrests. Points were scored by Laker because he undertook to stock spare parts at staging airports along the routes, to reduce delays when the aircraft broke down, as they did inevitably and regularly. This did not cost him much, but it did impress the military brass. Laker won his way into what was, in the mid-1950s, a profitable business.

He used low fares to get round IATA in earlier years, too. In 1952, Laker's company, Air Charter, muscled in on a scheme devised by Hunting, which was unable to carry it off. In those days, routes within the Commonwealth were outside IATA's pretty rigid control when it came to fares. So what had been dreamed up was called a colonial coach service. The British Government imposed all sorts of restrictions to protect the state-owned BOAC, but Laker was permitted to operate slow, twin-engined Vikings to Nairobi. It took around three days, against BOAC's typical timetable of a day or so. But the cheap, non-IATA service cost £98 one-way compared with £140 on BOAC. It proved to be very popular and within a month of starting up, the service was booked solidly for six months ahead. When Laker tried to improve things by moving up to quicker aircraft, the Government blocked it. It was this service that Laker later developed, using VC-10 jets, when he was with BUA, though the Government still prevented the service from carrying first-class passengers, to protect BOAC. However, it was a slightly different story when BUA took over the loss-making South American routes from BOAC in 1964. The state-owned carrier had declared that the routes were uneconomic without a government subsidy, which was refused. BUA grabbed the routes, using modified VC-10s, but it took a great deal of hard work to turn loss into profit. Laker had to persuade the monopolistic-minded South Americans to let BUA in at all. Then it was a matter of cutting BOAC's unnecessarily grand operation down to size to meet a stricter budget. It worked.

After he started his own airline, Laker several times absorbed surplus aircraft capacity by negotiating a lease-style deal with a foreign country. The aircraft would be painted in that country's national colours, thus providing her with an instant airline complete with flight crews. One of the first of these deals was with the Zambians, who leased one of his spare BAC 1-11s. He made a similar arrangement with Barbados, using a Boeing 707 that was made idle after he had been blocked from flying charters to the United States. Later, Laker Airways substituted surplus DC-10s. The services were flown as Caribbean Airways and Laker 'gave' the Barbados Government 51 per cent of the operation in 1973, when Caribbeanization was required and the operation was nominated as the national airline. Laker still used these aircraft from time to time, when capacity was needed for Laker Airways' own operations. Caribbean Airways' routes were loss-making ones, and after the bankruptcy they were taken over by British Caledonian (BCal).

One of the most profitable of these subcontracts was with Flug Union of West Berlin, flying package tourists away from the encircled city. This agreement began in 1967 and was still going, using an Airbus, at the very end, in 1982.

4 · The battle for take-off

Between 1970 and 1976, when Laker was fighting for Skytrain, the aviation policy of the British Government (and the party in power) changed and developed. Britain also went through major upheavals in her aviation relations with the United States, notably in the aftermath of the 1973-4 OPEC oil price increases. The fuel crisis led to an Anglo-American agreement to limit capacity on the North Atlantic, which in turn led to Britain later denouncing the Bermuda Agreement that covered air services between the two countries and had existed since 1946. The British goal behind this high-handed ending to a long-standing treaty was to substitute a more restrictive agreement that favoured British carriers. On top of this was Laker's effort to persuade the regulators, and later the courts, to grant permission for him to operate his Skytrain.

The foundation for Britain's modern aviation policy lies in the Civil Aviation Act that the Conservatives, under Harold Macmillan, passed in 1960, creating the Air Transport Licensing Board (ATLB) to regulate civil aviation. One of its aims was to give independent operators a bigger slice of the cake. Duncan Sandys, who was Minister of Aviation at the time, pursued a single-minded policy of enforced mergers between the large numbers of British aviation companies in order to produce, he hoped, stronger ones better able to compete in world markets. The Tories more obviously succeeded with the aerospace manufacturers because the Government held most of their purse strings. Out of these, two groups emerged: British Aircraft Corporation, mostly Vickers, English Electric (which was then in difficulty with the TSR-2), and later Bristol; and Hawker Siddeley, which absorbed Avro, Blackburn, Folland, and De Havilland (which was still in a precarious state following the Comet disasters). Handley Page would not go along meekly with this policy and later succumbed as a result of being starved of government business.

Similar 'encouragement' to the independent airlines was backed with two weapons. The newly created ATLB could specifically discriminate in favour of airlines with strong balance sheets. And the Government gradually shifted from arbitrarily handing out troop-carrying contracts on a buggins-turn basis—intended to divide the carriers against their own kind and so let the Defence Ministry rule. This had only succeeded in making a potentially profitable business barely solvent. Instead, contracts were to be given to the favoured few. The application of this new policy led directly to the formation of BUA, from Airwork and Hunting Clan.

In 1964 the Labour Party succeeded the Tories and began to question the 1960 Aviation Act. 'Too vague' was how Roy Jenkins, the new Minister of Aviation, put it. And after years of fudging things as it went along, the Labour Government eventually set up a major review committee in 1967. It is not clear whether the Cabinet hoped the inquiry would come out quite as clearly in favour of some measure of competition between the airlines as it did. But if the Wilson Government did not, then it should not have chosen as the committee's chairman Sir Ronald Edwards, chairman at the time of the Beecham Group, and former head of the Electricity Council and an economist. The inquiry's general line, however, certainly fitted in with the views of the late Tony Crosland, who was President of the Board of Trade and in charge of aviation, when the report was published in May 1969.

The Edwards report marked a watershed in British aviation politics. It drew a great deal of inspiration from Californian experience, where rigid control by the state utilities commission, over fares and how many carriers could fly a route, had benefited the consumer enormously through low fares all round. This same Californian experience later played a large part in encouraging the United States to adopt the policy of deregulating its domestic airlines.

Of the Edwards report's main recommendations, one had immediate impact. It read:

That the private sector should be encouraged to create a 'second force' airline, which should be licensed to operate a viable network [of routes], covering scheduled and inclusive tour/charter traffic. Where it is decided to license a second British operator on a route it should be this 'second force' airline. It must be financially and managerially strong, should embrace more than one of the existing airlines and will probably take time to arrange. Viability will require some limited concession of [nationalized] corporation territory. In exchange, and according to the size of the concession, the [proposed] National Air Holdings Board should be entitled to take a stake ... and to appoint one or more directors to the 'second force'.

The obvious candidate as claimant to centre stage in this second force should have been BUA. Under Freddie Laker's direction it had been built into an international carrier, with routes to East Africa and South America. It also had some routes into Europe. But since he had left, the group's basic weakness had reasserted itself: Laker and his chairman Wyatt had never managed to push the myriad of companies that made up the BUA group into anything approaching a cohesive whole.

From making profits when Laker was still managing director, the group's airline activities began to lose money on an increasing scale, over £1 million a year by 1969. Even before Laker's chair had cooled three major shareholders—Hunting Aviation, merchant banker Guinness Mahon, and shipping group Blue Star—dumped their stock, totalling a little over one-third. Cost-cutting exercises led to strikes, some of them nasty. The largest remaining shareholder, the Cayzer family, through its British and Commonwealth Shipping Group, began to prepare the airline business for sale. It paid all the other shareholders £16 million for the airline routes, a majority holding in Bristow Helicopters and BUA's various holdings in African airlines.

Sir Nicholas Cayzer's first move was to offer the long-haul and regional operations of BUA to British European Airways (BEA) for £9 million. Given the split of long- and short-haul operations between BEA and BOAC—and the likelihood that Labour would one day try to merge the two state-owned airlines—that plan was flawed from the start. BEA politely turned down the offer. Sir Nicholas trimmed the public price to £8·7 million, then offered BUA to BOAC.

In the background, the Scottish-based Caledonian was also gearing up to make a bid for BUA. No sooner had there been a meeting between Caledonian's Adam Thomson and Sir Nicholas than stories that a deal had already been agreed between BUA and BOAC appeared in the newspapers, leaked by an over-anxious BOAC. The price had come down, too, to £7·9 million, and the stories confidently asserted that Roy Mason, the President of the Board of Trade and therefore in charge of British aviation policy, had been asked to give his blessing by the end of March 1970. On the understanding that there had been no possibility of a merger with any other independent airline, and so complying with the main thrust of the Edwards report's recommendation, Mr Mason did not wait. The deal between BUA and BOAC was approved and Parliament informed.

Laker promptly made a fairly unlikely bid for BUA, which gained him some publicity and several brickbats from some trade union leaders. Clive Jenkins, leader of the Association of Scientific, Technical and Managerial Staffs and a long-standing Laker-hater, said Laker was nothing more than 'an old film star trying to make a comeback'. Laker didn't come back for a second dose.

A furious Caledonian management applied for all of BUA's route licences, which tied things up in a potential legal battle, and then counter-leaked that it had been very close to doing a deal with BUA. By the middle of the month a fine old parliamentary row had developed. On 18 March an embarrassed Roy Mason had to tell the Commons that he had been misled by Sir Nicholas and that the deal with BOAC was off until other bids could be considered. The Tories held their fire and withdrew a censure motion.

By the middle of May, when the new deadline for bids was up, Caledonian was the only serious bidder and it picked up BUA for £6·9 million. It also purchased three BAC 1-11s from British and Commonwealth Shipping for £5 million. On the face of it, Laker appeared to get less than nothing out of this rearrangement. And, for some time, that was the case.

The newly formed British Caledonian, created with official government blessing, wasted little time. It prepared an application for a ten-year licence to fly Gatwick–New York. Adam Thomson, BCal's chairman, wanted to turn the new airline into a full scheduled carrier. Within two years of its formation, it had been given a licence and a parallel designation with BOAC to fly as a British carrier to New York and Los Angeles. BCal also received permission to match BOAC's routes to Toronto and to Bahrain and Singapore. But having begun operations to New York and Los Angeles, BCal dropped both routes like hot potatoes in November 1974, when traffic fell off after the oil price shock. During 1974-5, BCal came near to going broke, sacked 15 per cent of its staff and cut many flights from its schedule. It was against this background of official encouragement for BCal that Laker had to persuade first the British Government and then that of the United States, that Skytrain should also be allowed to fly.

Laker's first application to the British ATLB was made in June 1971, a year after the Conservatives had come back into power with Edward Heath as Prime Minister. The ATLB was in a fairly weak-kneed state; the Edwards report had also recommended replacing it with what became the Civil Aviation Authority (CAA). The Tories from the first were expected to go along with Edwards. In fact, even under the latter part of the Wilson Government, the ATLB had been overruled, notably when it had leant so far in the direction of helping the independent airlines that it might have damaged either the state-owned BOAC or BEA.

And so it proved. The Tories, in their Civil Aviation Act of 1971, pushed the two nationalized airlines into a merger, which was never made to work (and which was officially undone in 1982). The 1971 Act duly replaced the ATLB with the CAA and obliged it to

> secure that at least one major British airline which is not controlled by the British Airways Board has opportunities to participate in providing, on charter or other terms, air transport services ... which satisfy all substantial categories of public demand (so far as British airlines may reasonably be expected to provide such services) at the lowest charges consistent with ... safety and an economic return. ...

At about this time, and just as Laker Airways was making its first licence application for Skytrain, IATA was tearing itself apart over how to compete with charters on the North Atlantic routes. The BOAC part of the newly formed British Airways was working hard to persuade the rest of the cartel that its idea for advance purchase fares (APEX) was the best direction to follow. These fares would fill otherwise unused (wasted) seats on scheduled services at marginal prices. Computer predictions of when seats could be expected to be available would be used to work out when to sell these cheaper seats. Other IATA carriers were predictably unimpressed. There was an unenthusiastic reaction from the Germans, French and Swiss, but the American carriers also were unmoved. IATA's way of fixing fares in this pre-Laker era was designed to protect the smallest and least efficient carriers (not always the same thing). This arose from what had been a long-standing rule in the club that required any vote on a fare or tariff to be unanimous, to prevent the lesser carriers from being swamped by the larger ones. A standard joke was that the cartel prevented competition between carriers to such a degree that the members measured the size of the chicken pieces in the sandwiches.

This period saw a build-up of massive overcapacity on the international air routes, and on the North Atlantic in particular. Boeing had developed the first widebodied jet, the 747 jumbo, which had 385 seats compared with the 185 of the Boeing 707s that they replaced. Pan Am had launched the 747 with an order for twenty-five and every other long-haul carrier rushed to place its own orders so as not to be left behind. There was a 24 per cent increase in the capacity flown on the North Atlantic in 1971, while the average number of seats filled that year fell to 50 per cent from 55 per cent in 1970. The industry had also seen a sharp increase in the number of passengers using charter services. America had its own problem with charters, or supplementals as they are known. The US Government had encouraged their growth by giving them lucrative contracts to carry the armed forces across the Pacific to the Vietnam war. That conflict was starting to wind down, yet the Government in Washington wanted to preserve the supplementals in case they were needed elsewhere in Asia.

It was a tough time for any new type of competitive service, such as Skytrain, to persuade officialdom to give it a break, especially when the established airlines were losing huge amounts of money without any extra competition. It was at this time that the mighty Pan Am nearly went bankrupt.

The best that even BOAC had been able to negotiate with IATA—and then through the British CAA—was an experiment with a form of APEX fare called Earlybird. But this applied only to their Bermuda route, which, because Bermuda is under British aegis, is free of US restrictions on the types of air fares that can be offered. Ray Colegate at the Board of Trade, who acted as liaison between the Edwards committee and the BoT (and who later moved to the CAA where he played a key part in Skytrain's development), came up with a modified version for charter carriers. Called ABC, for advance booking charters, it was intended to clean up the nonsensical rules over affinity groups. However, both the APEX and ABC fares required lengthy advance purchase periods, in some cases nearly two months, plus minimum stays. They did not match what Skytrain was supposed to do: create an instant-booking, walk-on charter for what Laker called the 'forgotten man', ignored by the scheduled carriers.

ATLB's inability to make a clear decision on Skytrain was fairly predictable. It said the debate over North Atlantic fares was 'too delicately balanced' to allow any guesses about the effect of Skytrain on the rest of the business. Nobody had any clear idea how many passengers, who would otherwise have flown on a normal scheduled carrier, would 'divert' to Skytrain. At this stage Laker reckoned there would be few. He still barely accepted the general view that Skytrain was likely to be seen by governments not as a special form of charter service but as a scheduled operation. While actually damning Skytrain, the ATLB also gave it faint praise. A trial might be worthwhile, it said, to solve the problem of illegal charters.

The following April, 1972, the newly formed CAA acquired its first full-time chairman, Lord Boyd-Carpenter, a former Tory Cabinet Minister. The appointment was a consolation prize for not being given the post of Speaker of the House of Commons, which had gone to Selwyn Lloyd. But Boyd-Carpenter's free-market leanings in time proved to be a blessing for Laker.

Despite the changes in official machinery, Laker appealed, saying that he could still get Skytrain into service (if approved) by August 1972. The CAA commissioner taking the appeal, Sir Dennis Proctor, was an ex-civil servant who had gone into industry. If Laker wanted to lose money on a Skytrain experiment—he had made it clear at the initial hearing that this wouldn't bankrupt the entire company—that was up to him, said Sir Dennis. The potential market was clearly there, according to the commissioner, who upheld Laker's appeal and put the ball firmly back into the Government's court.

British Airways, which was still trying to push APEX, its own answer to charter fares, paused only to question whether Skytrain would be profitable. It did not, however, object to it. But BCal did. The last thing it wanted while preparing its own effort to operate on the North Atlantic was any competitive interference.

On the ground that the CAA was new, and should therefore have the chance to hear the Skytrain case from the start, the Tory Government reversed Laker's win on appeal. John Davies, a former head of Shell Oil UK and of the Confederation of British Industry, was in charge of aviation policy. He was also head of a new Department made up of the former Industry and Trade Departments, giving him an impossibly wide brief and a very heavy workload. The views of, and advice from, officials during this period carried even more weight than usual. The civil servants were no supporters of Laker. Even though the Prime Minister eventually became involved, when Laker went to Downing Street on Maundy Thursday to ask for his help, Edward Heath reluctantly went along with putting the matter back to the CAA. There, a hearing lasting three days took place in August 1972.

Lord Boyd-Carpenter's interest in encouraging competition among the established airlines, and of putting a finger in IATA's eye, soon became apparent. He quickly asked Laker and his lawyers to define the traffic being aimed at, the profitability of such low fares (then proposed to be £32.50 one-way in winter and £37.50 one-way in summer—a saving of 37 per cent on IATA's cheapest fares), and how much diversion there would be from the scheduled carriers.

Laker wriggled on the question of diversion. 'Obviously it would be ridiculous for me to make a total statement that there will be no diversion ... I am saying that it is my considered opinion that there will be no measurable diversion with Skytrain.' He pointed out that the Icelandic airline, Loftleidir, had built up a 3 per cent share of the North Atlantic market on the basis of cheap fares (passengers had to put up with a stopover at Reykjavik on the way across the Atlantic). No scheduled carrier claimed that the quarter of a million or so passengers had been diverted from them. BCal nevertheless stepped up its protests that it would lose traffic to Skytrain.

As for the 'forgotten man'—or Laker's 'Identikit' as Boyd-Carpenter put it—he was defined in 1971–2 terms as a typical semi-skilled or skilled manual worker, earning £1,500 a year in Britain and \$7,000–\$8,000 in America. Laker estimated that there were millions of them, and that the market was a bottomless barrel. In 1971, 3 million travellers used charter flights on the North Atlantic, so Laker reckoned that there had to be 200,000 who needed to use his instant-booking, requirement-free Skytrain. That was all that was needed to make the service profitable.

He knew that if he made Skytrain too simple, he would stand no chance of getting official approval for it. There were limits to how much competition for the established airlines even the likes of Boyd-Carpenter would tolerate. Clearly there would be a risk of diversion from the scheduled carriers. Laker explained the problem and his solution to it:

> We had to propose a service that would cater to the genuine quick-ticket man and yet put a sufficient artificial barrier in his way that it would not divert traffic from scheduled services. And this is where the no-reservations idea came from. This is the artificial barrier that we dreamed up.

Business travellers would want firm advance bookings to be sure of getting to their destinations on time. Outside the hearings, he admitted that there were no statistics to prove that the potential Skytrain market actually existed. It was a market that 'does not now fly,' he maintained. 'We'll soon know. At the end of two months flying Skytrain we will be able to tell you whether it is a success or a complete and utter failure.'

On the matter of Skytrain's profitability, there had been another twist since the first hearing. Through his knack of being in the right place at the right time, Laker had been offered DC-10s at a bargain price through the Japanese trading company, Mitsui. If he could fill an average of 180 seats a flight on the DC-10 throughout the year, against the 119 average load for the Boeing 707s that he had originally planned to use, the larger widebodied jet would break even. Laker's optimistic style suggested that this would be no problem. Any passenger carried above the break-even level would be even more profitable on the DC-10, he argued, since it was a newer and more efficient design, and its seat-mile cost (the total operating cost divided by the number of seats available) was lower. Even though the DC-10s on offer were of the short-range type, designed for use within the United States, Laker calculated that with careful operation they would have sufficient range for his routes. Mitsui was exposed to a Laker-style deal, as we shall see. The CAA voted Laker's way. It said:

> We accept the contention [by Laker] that there is a substantial demand for cheap, no-frills, short-notice, mass travel which is not presently adequately catered for. We welcome [Laker's] enterprise in seeking to meet this demand and we view with favour the innovation involved in this application.

But there were strings firmly attached. Laker had a ten-year licence for Skytrain from the British, starting on 1 January 1973. In the winter months, however, the capacity of the DC-10 had to be artificially restricted to that of the Boeing 707. Laker had also asked to fly from Gatwick, but the approval said that Skytrain would have to depart from Stansted, a charter field north-east of London with no rail link, appalling road connections and no scheduled services operating. And it was miles from Laker's Gatwick headquarters. The reason for this change of venue was simple: it was to stop Laker poaching other airlines' passengers with his attractive low fares. The advice from Laker's American lawyer Bob Beckman was to accept all the conditions, since 'they could always be negotiated away later.'

In February 1973, the British Government crowned the licence with the all-important designation under the Bermuda Agreement with the Americans. As far as Whitehall was concerned, Laker Airways' Skytrain service was all set to operate from London (Stansted) to New York. All that remained now was for Laker to convince Washington. That should have been a mere formality, since the Bermuda treaty required what was called 'reciprocity', which meant that the Americans had to accept whatever airline the British Government nominated from its end. The approval from Washington should therefore have been signed by the President without undue delay. Instead it turned out to be a whole new battle.

At this point, the Americans were less than keen on Skytrain. Their two major carriers on the North Atlantic, Pan Am and TWA, were losing heavily. And the supplementals, or charter operators, were even hungrier for business. Laker was also seen as an undesirable operator because of the many breaches of the affinity group charter rules. America's aviation authorities at the CAB gave Laker's Skytrain the thumbs down, though the decision was not made public. As it turned out, this never came to a head because of another change in British aviation policy. The Tories were swept out of power when Edward Heath decided to take on the popularity of the coal miners at the polls, and lost. Wilson's Labour Party was back in power, and Laker's free-market ideas and his Skytrain were about to become victims of Britain's lurch to the left.

5 · Between Bermuda 2 and the courts

While America deliberately dithered over the Skytrain application, the British Government vacillated. At the end of February 1973, Britain's Ambassador to the United States had sent to the CAB the necessary six copies of Laker's application for a permit together with a covering letter, in which he requested that 'processes associated with this designation be expedited to the maximum degree possible'.

The sticking point at the CAB was the matter of Laker's 'illegal' affinity group charters. The chief hawk at the CAB on this issue was Dick O'Melia, who held a rigid view of the rightness of things. US law had been broken as O'Melia saw it, and to clear the slate he required the biggest fine ever imposed, since Laker had been the carrier most obviously exposed. The demand was $101,000; Laker agreed to pay up in July. 'The fine represented something like one and a half flights to New York,' Laker said later. 'I agreed to confess under duress because I had an axe over my head.... It became a matter of whether to sell my pride for $101,000, or to put my company and staff, myself and our services to the public in jeopardy. Eventually I had my price,' he admitted, with obvious distaste. It took until March 1974 for a report to emerge from the administrative law judge at the CAB, Greer M. Murphy, who had held hearings in the intervening period. The judge backed Laker, saying: 'It was in the public interest to issue a licence to Laker Airways.' There the matter stuck yet again.

The CAB eventually recommended in June 1974 that President Nixon should refuse the licence because of Laker's 'conviction' over illegal charters—which was as good a way as any other of protecting the American carriers. The fact that a whole range of carriers (Japan Air Lines, Alitalia, Pan Am, TWA, British Airways—there were more than 130 cases in all) were also 'guilty' of contravening the rules by those criteria was apparently beside the point. It was Laker who wanted to do something competitively different.

During a ten-year period, the CAB collected almost $2 billion in fines, slightly more than half from American carriers (scheduled and charter). As a later Senate report put it:

> The Board has concentrated its enforcement efforts upon stopping improper low-cost travel; it has done so persistently and not always fairly. The result is public criticism of, and resentment against, the Board's enforcement policy.... The public wants low-cost travel; several airlines wish to provide low-cost travel; the Board's rules inhibit the provision of low-cost travel; the public is willing to violate those rules....

It was not only O'Melia, but the CAB as a whole that believed in what it was doing. In fact, O'Melia and Laker later became friends when Laker publicly supported O'Melia's nomination to membership of the Board itself. During the earlier part of this period the CAB had been chaired by Secor Browne, an advocate of protectionism, and then later by Robert Timm, a colourless bureaucrat who was eventually forced to resign because he became too close to the airline industry. The White House—and the rest of Washington—was in any case paralysed by the Watergate scandal, which had come to light in 1972. And on top of all this was America's humiliating withdrawal from Vietnam, which left the American aviation authorities with another problem: a large number of charter carriers that had grown on the back of carrying troops across the Pacific now had to be protected. All in all, it was not surprising that the White House simply sat on its hands over Laker's application to operate Skytrain. The fact that it was an astonishing, unilateral abrogation of a long-standing international aviation treaty (the Bermuda Agreement) was, relatively speaking, unimportant. Polite, even impolite, diplomatic pressure from the British failed to move things at all.

Back in London, the Secretary of State for Trade, Peter Shore, who was in charge of civil aviation, had more important things on his mind. The Labour Government was manoeuvring itself for the second general election within a year. The strategy was to woo the trade unions, and openly going out of his way to help anti-union Laker would do Shore no good at all. The overall strategy worked. The Labour Party was re-elected, increasing its overall majority to five.

In the meantime, the North Atlantic aviation trade was quietly being carved up with the open assistance of the US and British Governments. A process that had begun in 1974, it was being done in such a way that Laker's Skytrain would be permanently pigeon-holed. In the aftermath of OPEC's quadrupling of the oil prices, overall air traffic on the North Atlantic in 1974 declined by 8·5 per cent. Passengers carried by scheduled carriers went down 6 per cent, while charters fell by a disastrous 30 per cent (though accounting for only a small share of the total). Pan Am was bleeding to death; its chairman, Najeeb Halaby, had been ousted and replaced by Bill Seawell, who was himself ousted in 1981. America's flag carrier was surviving only by the day-to-day goodwill of its bankers. At one point it had seemed as though a stake in Pan Am was going to be sold to the Shah of Iran. The American authorities had already agreed to scme sharing of routes and a carve-up of capacity within the United States, in complete contradiction to their normal feelings about such breaches of anti-trust law. Now they agreed to work on carving up the North Atlantic where, with all the Boeing 747 jumbos that had been introduced by the major airlines, there was massive overcapacity. There was undoubtedly an emergency as far as the established carriers were concerned.

In mid-September 1974, talks between Pan Am, TWA, BA and BCal were held in the CAB's Washington offices, with observers from the CAA and British Embassy present. It soon became clear that if there was to be an agreed, uniform reduction of capacity, it would only occur provided Laker's Skytrain was not allowed to start on the route. The deal, announced by Peter Shore on 23 September, was for a one-fifth cut in the number of scheduled seats available between November 1974 and April 1975, compared with the same period a year earlier. Bill Waltrip of Pan Am (president until 1982), emphasized to the closed meeting that Skytrain—a fifth carrier—would 'automatically terminate the New York–London agreement'. And they were not objecting to Skytrain's presence merely during this winter period. Waltrip confirmed in answer to a question from BCal's Charles Powell that the deal would still be off even if Laker didn't start until the following summer or later. William Slattery of TWA agreed: 'We've been discussing a rational situation.... The advent of a fifth carrier makes this a kind of a nonsense.' When pressed by Ossie Cochran of BA, Waltrip went further. Not only would the New York–London deal be called off immediately, but the American carriers would also want to review any other agreed capacity cuts.

During the summer, the British Government had been making placatory noises to Laker, reassuring him that they were doing their best to persuade the Americans, though they were warning him loud and clear that he was not likely to get started during the coming winter. It was only after Laker's enterprising Washington lawyer used the US Freedom of Information Act to obtain a transcript of the capacity reduction meeting that Laker found out what had really been going on. He was just off on one of his publicity-seeking trips for his renamed Laker Air Travel tour business, when he was told the established airlines' private feelings towards Skytrain. In full view of a television crew from the BBC, he blasted at Britain's aviation civil servants who had connived against him, and called them 'bums and gangsters'. This was mild in comparison with his private thoughts at that time, but it was enough to alienate the top civil servant in charge of aviation, George Rogers, then an under-secretary at the Board of Trade. Rogers's views on aviation were strictly mercantilist, rigidly in favour of one airline from each country per international route, and fairly obviously anti-American to boot. He didn't like Laker and regarded Skytrain as an excrescence. Now Laker had no official support in either camp, London or Washington.

So for the first, and not the last, time in Skytrain's history, Laker turned to the courts. Almost exactly two years to the day after the British Government had designated Skytrain for London–New York, the carrier's American lawyer, Bob Beckman, filed in the US District Court in Washington DC writs claiming conspiracy to delay Skytrain and claiming around £7 million in damages, calculated at £17,000 a day for five months, which was about equal to the total investment in Skytrain at that time. (Soon after, Laker claimed that the total investment, including Mitsui's, had by this time reached £31 million.) Obviously, the writ referred to the capacity deal among Pan Am, TWA, BA and BCal that excluded

Laker, which none of them could deny existed. So the major carriers did a quick deal with Laker's lawyers; they rapidly withdrew the original agreement and rewrote it, so that it was in all essentials the same, but did not specifically exclude Laker Airways. That way, in theory, diplomatic pressure could still force the Americans to cough up Laker's overdue licence, which was what he really wanted.

Laker did not have to wait long for retaliation. As a Christmas present, on 23 December, British Airways applied to the CAA in London for the Skytrain licence to be revoked. The reason given on the application: circumstances had changed materially since the licence was first granted in 1972. Traffic was at best stagnant; fuel prices were rising; and existing carriers were suffering substantial losses. BA also claimed that low-fare traffic was being looked after through advance booking charters, though IATA was still keeping APEX fares on scheduled services in a box. The real reason was to keep sweet the group of established carriers that feared greatly that Laker Airways would add 500,000 seats a year to an already overcrowded route.

Lord Boyd-Carpenter's angry response to BA's claim took less than a month to appear after the CAA held hearings. On 5 February 1975, the application was rejected, pithily:

It would be wrong to render nugatory Laker Airways' expenditure so far of up to £7 million by going back on these decisions without the most compelling reasons.... We are conscious also that the only reason why Skytrain services have not already been in operation for the past two years is that the United States' authorities have engaged in unconscionable procrastination. Having long since exhausted the procedural opportunities for inaction that the CAB has at its disposal, the US authorities have sought final refuge in silence.... In sum, notwithstanding the weighty and well-argued case advanced by BA, we conclude that it would be wrong to revoke the licence.... We regard the Skytrain experiment as one to be launched in propitious circumstances when the operator and the public can have confidence that the experiment will prove successful.

BA had little hope of winning. By this time, BA had Frank McFadzean as its chairman (now Lord McFadzean, chairman of

Rolls-Royce), and he could not bring himself to launch an appeal against a competitor, despite the advice of his staff. BA had, however, achieved what it really wanted at that time, a delay in dealing with Skytrain. While all this was going on, there was no pressure (in fact the reverse) on Washington to approve Skytrain. The delay also gave time for the Labour Government to be persuaded to come to terms with the idea. And in late July 1975, what for a time seemed to be the *coup de grâce* for Skytrain was pronounced by Peter Shore.

Laker was relaxing on his 85-foot company yacht *Tutinella* in the Mediterranean, when he got an urgent call that Peter Shore wanted to see him at once. The aviation policy review, which had been announced almost immediately after the October 1974 general election, was now complete. When Laker got to Shore's office, the Secretary of State was flanked, among others, by George Rogers. Shore dropped his not totally unexpected bombshell. He was arranging to partition Britain's overseas airlanes between BA and BCal. There was no room for Skytrain, and so its designation, London to New York, was to be cancelled. Shore also said that Laker's licence would be revoked. Laker tried going through all his arguments in favour of Skytrain, but to no avail. As a last throw he asked to be allowed to operate a short Skytrain experiment. Shore turned to his officials who gave the thumbs down, and that was that. By government fiat, all Laker's work and investment were brought to nothing.

When Shore announced this complete reversal of policy to the Commons an hour later, he used every one of the arguments BA had used in its failed attempt to persuade the CAA to revoke Skytrain's licence, together with another one. The failure of BCal on both the New York and Los Angeles routes proved, he said, that times were too hard to allow any British competition for other British carriers on the international airways. BCal was to get its own private run to West Africa and South America. At this stage of the carve-up, BCal lost routes to New York, Los Angeles, Atlanta, Toronto, Houston and Bahrain–Singapore. But by the time the Government's White Paper emerged seven months later, BCal had won exclusive rights to serve the southern United States. Nobody in the Labour Government wanted to kill off BCal—and its almost 4,000 unionized jobs. And, no, said Shore to the Commons, he did not think he had been ruthless over Laker. A guest at the back of the obligatory press conference that followed was Laker, seething with righteous indignation. When Shore had finished, Laker had this to say: 'We still hold a licence. Any changes in the policy guidelines [to the CAA telling it to cancel Laker's licence] have to be approved by Parliament. Before they become law there has to be a debate. I will continue to be a buccaneer.' He then went on to affirm: 'I can assure Mr Shore and all who think like him that Skytrain will remain on the books until the day I die.' Laker also said he would go to court.

When the news reached Washington, officials rapidly extracted the CAB's negative decision on Skytrain from the White House. America had been relieved of the responsibility for blocking Skytrain. Peter Shore—encouraged by BA, BCal, Pan Am, TWA and his own officials—had done it for them.

How to turn the policy into fact? Technical legislative problems caused publication of the White Paper on the subject to be delayed from its planned date in the autumn until February 1976. The Government considered an amendment to the 1971 Civil Aviation Act, but parliamentary time was limited; there was already a legislative backlog. It could, Shore was advised by government lawyers, be achieved by issuing new guidance to the CAA to replace the mild and inoffensive Tory version of 1972. And this new guidance became the second half of the White Paper. As Laker already knew by the time of the Minister's July press conference, turning such guidance into law would require a vote of both Houses of Parliament, the Commons and the Lords.

Before the subsequent debates on the White Paper, Laker had consulted Margaret Thatcher, the new leader of the Tories. Her husband, Denis, and Freddie Laker had known each other for years, as they were both directors of the Castrol oil company. There was, she advised, little that could be done about the Commons; the whips would see to it that the Government won. But the Lords might be different. On the day, in order not to throw out the baby with the bathwater, the Lords, too, voted for the White Paper, but with a caveat; they also voted 83 to 68 calling on the Government to withdraw the instruction to the CAA to revoke the Skytrain licence. Peter Shore dithered, and promptly forgot the request.

It had taken time to find lawyers who gave Laker much of a chance in court, but eventually he did find a willing lawyer in

London and a writ was filed on 16 March, the day after the Lords had voted in his favour. The writ alleged that Peter Shore had acted beyond his legal powers in giving such guidance to the CAA that it should revoke the Skytrain licence. Before the verdict was released, another event occurred in this counterplay of governments, airlines and the courts that was tossing Laker around like a cork in a mill race. Edmund Dell had taken over as Secretary of State for Trade and so had inherited the mare's-nest that was Britain's current aviation policy. He is as different from Shore as chalk is from cheese. Shore is a left-winger; Dell's politics (for a former Labour Cabinet Minister) are often nearer to those of the Tories than of his own party. When he left politics Dell went to merchant bank Guinness Peat, which also happens to be heavily involved in financing the aviation business.

In spite of advice to the contrary from the Foreign Office and the Treasury, Dell agreed to go along with the wishes of officials in the BoT and, on 23 June 1976, gave one year's notice that the British Government was to denounce the 1946 Bermuda Agreement with the United States. The old treaty was a model used for many international bilateral aviation agreements around the world. In the intervening twelve months before it died, a new one was to be renegotiated. The matter of Skytrain and its potential involvement in this renegotiation simply did not come before Dell, since all his officials thought that Laker would lose hands down in the courts.

One of the causes of the British denunciation was the bickering that had developed between the US and British Governments over the 1974 capacity restraint deal that had put Laker on the wrong side of the fence, though not out of any concern for Laker. Traffic on the North Atlantic had picked up and the Americans wanted to return to business as usual. Capacity restraints were not part of Bermuda 1 but, having created the precedent, the British wanted them formally included as part of what had immediately become known as Bermuda 2. The British were agitated about the split of the North Atlantic aviation business between the two countries' territories. American carriers in the years to March 1976 earned $513 million, while British carriers earned just $223 million.

This 69:31 split had grown too wide for the British. One of George Rogers's special tricks to redress the balance was to call for single designation, meaning that only one airline from each country could fly on any route between the two countries. This suggestion was impossible for the Americans to agree to, since it would have meant either Pan Am or TWA giving up its right to fly London–New York. The British were also concerned (along with all other countries flying to the United States) about the increasingly unpredictable reaction by the CAB to fare proposals. The IATA cartel had filed, on 11 March 1976, for a fare increase for all international carriers on the North Atlantic for that summer. The CAB had waited until the afternoon of 30 April to block the increase; by that time in Washington it was already early evening in Europe.

The timing of the British move was, in part at least, designed to take advantage of the expected confusion in Washington during the presidential election, which eventually led to a change of President. It is one of those interesting, but useless, speculations to wonder just how far the British would have succeeded with their policy if they had been ready to denounce Bermuda 1 a year or so earlier, when the Americans were still mesmerized by the after-effects of the Watergate mess and, in aviation specifically, by Pan Am's financial woes. As it turned out, the British side did much better in the renegotiations than might at first have been expected.

In a bitter blow for Peter Shore, for the Trade Department's civil servants, and especially for the Department's lawyers, Laker scored a crushing victory in late July with his court case. Mr Justice Mocatta, sitting in the Queen's Bench Division, came down entirely on Laker's side. The Secretary of Sate had acted *ultra vires*, beyond his powers. The Judge swept aside all economic arguments about Skytrain and its potential effect on other carriers.

> Those arguments could not be resolved with certainty without either the gift of prophecy or putting the matter to the test by allowing Skytrain to operate; and in so far as the judgment of a court could be said to be capable of determining what would happen in the future, they could be solved only after a long and careful hearing outside the function of the court.

The outcome of the case turned on the wording of the guidance given in the Tories' Civil Aviation Act of 1971, summarized earlier (see page 34), and how this tied in with paragraphs seven and eight of the guidance section of Shore's White Paper, the key parts of which said:

In the case of long-haul scheduled services ... the CAA should not ... license more than one British airline to serve the same route.... The CAA should review existing licences and exemptions in the light of this paragraph and take appropriate action.... Another carrier could be licensed if the carrier with that sphere of influence [i.e. BA or BCal] gave its consent.

A special section of the White Paper's guidance spelled out what this meant for Laker and Skytrain. In part, it said: 'The Secretary of State has decided that Laker Airways' designation as a scheduled service operator under the United Kingdom/United States Air Services Agreement [Bermuda 1] should be cancelled.'

Mr Justice Mocatta's view was that the Shore direction to the CAA, that there should only be one carrier, was clearly outside Shore's powers. 'It was plainly a direction which drastically altered the duty conferred on the CAA.' The fact that another airline might be allowed to fly if BA or BCal gave their consent did not, in Mr Justice Mocatta's view, 'remove the vice of the direction. If anything it aggravated it. To say to the CAA that it must not even consider granting a licence on a route already served by either of the named airlines without their consent was to impose a fetter, apparently intended to be absolute....' This went way beyond the ambit of the term 'guidance' in the basic Act. The fact that both Houses of Parliament had voted to approve the White Paper was no defence either; only a statute can amend a statute, the Judge declared.

The Government had also claimed that, as the Crown, it had royal prerogative over both designating an airline and later revoking that designation. This, Mr Justice Mocatta said, was a more difficult issue. For several reasons—the terms of the Act and Skytrain's licence under it, the refusal by the CAA in early 1975 to revoke the licence when asked (and the lack of an appeal from the state-owned carrier), and the provisions of the original and still operating Bermuda 1 Agreement—the Judge sided with Laker again. The Act did restrict the Crown's prerogative over revoking the designation. The Government was not entitled to withdraw the designation until its ten-year term ran out on 31 December 1982, or the licence was legally removed by the CAA, or the Bermuda Agreement ended, which the Government had decided was to happen in June 1977. It seemed they had Laker, coming or going.

The Government said it would appeal. The Attorney-General, Sam Silkin, was particularly unhappy about losing on a matter of the Crown's prerogative. A date was set for the appeal to be heard in late November.

In the meantime, the negotiations with the Americans over a revised Bermuda 2 treaty were not going well for the British. The lack of a detailed, well-prepared case, and George Rogers's uncompromising attitude, had bogged matters down. The Americans refused to budge over the question of single designation and they were scathing when there were no ready answers to straightforward questions as to market shares and the like. And so came more change. The United States decided it was time to upgrade the negotiations. They appointed to head their side a special ambassador, Alan Boyd, a former US Secretary of Transportation (and until the summer of 1982 the head of Amtrak). The British considered matching this with a special ambassador of their own, but instead put Patrick Shovelton in charge. He was an under-secretary, outranking Rogers by one all-important grade. After Shovelton had finished helping Britain negotiate her way into the EEC, he had been employed sweeping up trouble spots in the Industry and Trade Departments. His previous experience included international shipping negotiations (he now heads the British Shipping Council). The negotiations over Bermuda 2 took a more positive turn.

Before very much could be agreed—the two sides were still miles apart on major issues, especially over single designation and capacity controls—on 15 December the Court of Appeal came out with its verdict, from the mouth of the Master of the Rolls, Lord Denning, who had heard the case with Lords Justice Roskill and Lawton. Even now, Patrick Shovelton can recall almost verbatim the first paragraph of Lord Denning's judgment, giving a fair imitation of his Lordship's Hampshire burr. From the first short sentence, Shovelton knew that the Department, and the Government, had lost.

Mr Laker is a man of enterprise. He has an exciting project for travel by air. He wishes to start a new air service across the North Atlantic from England to the United States. It is to be quite unlike conventional air services. It is to be more like a railway service. Passengers are not to reserve their seats in advance.

They are to go to the airport, buy their tickets and board the aircraft—all in one sequence—just as passengers go to a railway station, buy their tickets, and join the train. So Mr Laker calls his project Skytrain. He hopes to attract a hitherto untapped source of traffic. He is going to cut out all the travel agents and their expensive commissions. He is going to charge fares much lower than other carriers. He is not going to fly from Heathrow, but from Stansted; so there are no in-transit facilities. By these measures he suggests that he will not take away traffic from the established airlines, but will create new custom. He will carry passengers who would not otherwise have travelled at all.

Much more followed, but by now everybody knew where Lord Denning's sympathies lay.

There is one strange aspect to the judgment. All along, Lord Denning assumed that the United States' CAB had recommended that Skytrain be approved, whereas it is now clear that the reverse was the case. Had the CAB's true position been known, it would have left the way open for Secretary of State Edmund Dell to use the section of the Civil Aviation Act of 1971 that Lord Denning said specifically would' have been a valid means of stopping Skytrain. This section allows the Secretary of State to give orders to the CAA that have to be obeyed, in times of war, national emergency, or in 'any matter appearing ... to affect the relations of the UK with another country'. If there was a proper case for stopping Skytrain, said Lord Denning (and the impasse over the Bermuda 2 negotiations with America provided a perfect excuse), this section of the Act provided a 'perfectly good means' of doing so. And in such a case, there would have been no inquiry of any sort.

Laker's case even referred to a precedent set in 1611, when King James I attempted to govern by making proclamations, and Sir Edward Coke declared that the King had no prerogative but that which the law of the land allowed him. The same was true now, argued Lord Denning; the Civil Aviation Act controlled the prerogative of the Secretary of State. His prerogative was to persuade Parliament to change the statute, something that had in fact been considered at the start of all this and rejected by the government lawyers as unnecessary. As Edmund Dell now recalls, not one of these lawyers at any stage gave Laker's chances in court a prayer. But they had been wrong about Laker's legal position from the start. The Attorney-General, Sam Silkin, was desperately worried about losing again on the issue of the Crown's prerogative. He asked, and was immediately granted, leave to appeal to the House of Lords, Britain's highest court.

And so Laker's Skytrain suddenly became a crucial political issue. Should the Government appeal to the Lords and risk further humiliation, or accept the drubbing already handed down, and give way? If it did concede, then Skytrain would become a key pawn in the negotiations over Bermuda 2 with the Americans. They were refusing point blank to accept that Skytrain was a special form of charter service, instead insisting that it be treated as a scheduled carrier. And that fitted exactly into the debate over single or double designation. BCal was no longer a candidate for London–New York (Los Angeles was being quietly ignored at this point). Britain was going to have to accept Pan Am and TWA on London–New York. Skytrain could become the second British carrier alongside BA. The pseudo-econometrics, amounting to little more than guesswork, that had predicted that Skytrain would cost BA £3 million a year—plus another £3 million a year for each American rival allowed to fly the transatlantic route—was all promptly ignored. The final decision over whether or not to appeal to the Lords was, however, made on more practical political grounds than that.

The Prime Minister, James Callaghan, had a habit of silencing Edmund Dell at Cabinet meetings—telling him to be quiet because he knew nothing of politics. Dell, who from the start could not see why Laker should be prevented from running Skytrain, in this instance riposted that Laker was now more popular than ever, and 'wasn't that what politics were supposed to be about?' Dell also rejected absolutely that he should take Lord Denning's advice and use the foreign policy exemption built into the Act. 'It would have been politically impossible, having lost, to pull a new rabbit from the hat,' Dell explained.

Against the neat link with the Bermuda 2 negotiations, and Laker's popularity with the British public at large, was to be weighed the resentment of the trade unions. This was an era in Britain of so-called voluntary incomes policy, when the unions agreed to hold wages down a little in return for government favours. It was also a time when a major opinion poll had clearly shown that the country's top union leader, Jack Jones of the Transport and General Workers Union, was regarded in Britain as by far the most influential man in the country. A turning point in the Cabinet debate over the Laker appeal came through Shirley Williams, who was the Minister in charge of price-control policy. She sided with Dell in favour of Laker and of introducing some competition in the airlanes.

There was a further, and wholly British, justification for backing Laker, as Dell spelled out in a speech after he had left government. Switching policies and endorsing Laker, he said, 'would be a nice card to play against the USA, which previously had refused to admit Skytrain. They would now be forced to admit it if they were not to drain all credibility from their consumerist propaganda, propaganda they loved to use when they themselves felt competitive.'

The legal question over prerogative was finally settled in the light of a judgment made the previous year, when the Lords had ruled on appeal that the Education Secretary, Fred Mulley, had acted *ultra vires* on the volatile question of enforced comprehensive education. In the Laker appeal, Lord Denning pointedly cited this case, and added further emphasis. 'It is a serious matter for the courts to declare that a Minister of the Crown has exceeded his powers. So serious that we think hard before doing it. But there comes a point when it has to be done,' he solemnly warned. After a cooling-off period Attorney-General Sam Silkin took the hint. There was to be no appeal. Thus ended one of the most extraordinary periods in British government in modern times.

Laker was free and clear; Skytrain still had its licence and its designation from the British for London–New York, and Los Angeles was clearly up for grabs. On 18 February 1977, the British Government made a virtue of necessity, conceded the inevitable and agreed to double designation on routes to New York and Los Angeles. And so the British Embassy in Washington restarted the process to get Laker an American permit. It was given immediate approval. As we'll see later, the view on aviation policy under President Carter was going to be quite different from that of his Republican predecessors. Laker's only problem now might be the eventual outcome of the Bermuda 2 negotiations.

The Americans were still pushing for more freedom for carriers to compete than under Bermuda 1; the British for less. There was much bullying to advance one viewpoint or another. President Carter twice telephoned Callaghan on the matter, threatening that air services between the United States and Britain would be cut off on the deadline day if a suitable deal were not concluded. Callaghan always deferred to Dell, who made reassuring noises and declared that air services would not actually be cut off. However, Dell was not entirely sure, and would have had to resign if things had gone wrong. Brock Adams, the US Secretary of Transportation (a bumptious man with a loud voice), made a series of threats 'every time he opened his mouth' according to the British side. As the deadline, midnight, 21 June 1977, approached, the airlines flying the North Atlantic between Britain and the United States began to advertise emergency plans. British Airways would fly people to and from Canada and then arrange connections from there, while American carriers proposed to divert their flights to continental airports, such as Brussels and Schiphol, Amsterdam.

In the end, of course, the pressure forced the negotiators to come to some conclusion. Alan Boyd's nerve cracked first. As a political appointee to the job he was on less secure ground than Shovelton, and he later dropped out of the aviation scene, having to take much criticism as he went. His inclinations tended more towards the British protectionist view than to the pro-competitive stance of his new Carterite masters in Washington.

There had been much prodding from Washington to get the job finished on time and so solve this conflict with the British. Right from the start of the Bermuda 2 negotiations, Britain's Ambassador in Washington, Sir Peter Ramsbotham, had persistently warned that it was 'fouling up UK–US relations' in general. Somehow, aviation matters, for all their minor importance in the scale of things, tend to occupy a disproportionate amount of political time. The deal was a good one for Britain, thanks to astute negotiating by Shovelton, who was not averse to dragging Americans off to play golf at tricky moments, or arranging long, elaborate lunches to break the opposition's concentration. The deal was not finally concluded until five o'clock on the morning of 22 June, well after the deadline, and then only by agreeing to disagree on some of the details until wrap-up talks in July. Immediately the outline agreement had been initialled, section by section, by Shovelton and Boyd, the American side rushed to the telephone to tell Washington. The American authorities had prepared the paperwork to cancel all British permits and it was already 10 a.m. in Washington.

The British did not achieve single designation on any routes except to New York and Los Angeles. During the first three years of the new Agreement, several new gateways (entry airports) within the United States were added: Atlanta and Dallas–Fort Worth for American carriers, and Houston for BCal. BA was to be allowed to fly non-stop to San Francisco and to Seattle. With other existing points (London to Boston, Chicago, Detroit, Miami, Philadelphia and Washington), together with another one to be chosen later by the Americans, there were in all to be fourteen gateways into the United States. The Americans lost most of their fifth-freedom rights, that is, the right to stop in London on the way to or from another country and to pick up or put down passengers. They retained only West Germany and West Berlin (a special case) in Europe, but gained a prize in the East in the shape of a new right to fly fifth-freedom traffic from Hong Kong to Singapore. Capacity controls were finally forced on the Americans by Shovelton, though they were looser than he had hoped for. Within the overall aim of keeping average load factors on the North Atlantic to at least 65 per cent, each side was allowed to add extra flights. The travel boom that had already begun by the time these negotiations were completed saw to it that for the first few years the 65 per cent figure was easily met with the addition of many extra flights. The British played the rule flexibly. But in the weak market of 1981–2 that helped to kill Laker Airways, even with flights cut back, load factors fell. The British reverted to type and began to make use of the restrictions they had negotiated into the Bermuda 2 treaty.

There was just one other twist in the Bermuda 2 story as far as Laker was concerned. In order to boost Gatwick Airport and to relieve some of the appalling congestion at Heathrow, the British were trying to persuade airlines to switch. The established majors refused, since there were far fewer interline connections at Gatwick, making it less convenient for their long-haul passengers. So the British announced that all new American carriers serving newly added gateways under Bermuda 2 (e.g., Delta from Atlanta and Braniff from Dallas–Fort Worth) would have to use Gatwick. To make this policy uniform, the British had little choice but also to switch Laker's Skytrain from Stansted to Gatwick. This was the final element in turning it into a fully competitive scheduled service, albeit at first with just one class of passenger and no advance booking.

With all sorts of restrictions over where and when tickets might be sold, Laker by now also had his American permit. After six years, three court cases and umpteen appearances at the CAA and CAB, the real battle facing Laker and his Skytrain was about to begin.

The first shots were fired even before his first flight. Laker had always been concerned that he would not be allowed even a short period of monopoly for the Skytrain type of service. He, and a lot of other people in the aviation business, anticipated that one of the American supplementals would announce a copy-cat version of Skytrain. Instead the competition came from the scheduled carriers on the North Atlantic: Pan Am, TWA and BA.

In mid-August, IATA announced a package of three fares designed to compete with Skytrain, and all at about the same fare. They were: a Budget fare, to be booked 21 days in advance with the airline having the freedom to select the exact day on which the passenger flew (to fill empty seats); an APEX fare, booked between 45 and 50 days in advance (soon reduced to 21 days); and a Standby fare, sold only on the day of the flight. The prospect, Laker later confessed, 'scared me half to death'.

6 · A paternalistic boss

Laker's beliefs are the absolute antithesis of everything the Labour Party stands for. Not only is he a free-wheeling entrepreneur, out to do battle with the nationalized airlines, but he also cannot stand dealing with trade unions and doesn't care who knows. Yet the Callaghan Labour Government managed to turn a Nelsonian eye towards Laker Airways' consistent refusal even to consider negotiating with the unions, which were for ever trying to get their foot in its door.

Laker's feelings about trade unions go back a long way. When he was head of BUA he had no choice but to deal with the unions, since they were already recognized at Airwork, the founding company of the independent carrier. He had to withstand many bitter strikes and went out of his way to be abrasive to trade union leaders. During several strikes, management staff routinely took over striking workers' jobs. During one strike, by BUA's maintenance engineers, Laker managed to persuade some of the official inspectors from the Air Registration Board to come in at night to carry out their checks that things were being done properly. On another occasion, non-union management staff also took over as cleaners when the regulars went on strike. As one of Laker's closest aides said: 'You were not fully initiated into the management until you had been christened by the dewdrop trolley'—which means making an unfortunate error while emptying an aircraft's lavatory catch tank.

Just before the first Skytrain went into service in September 1977, the Transport and General Workers Union persuaded the government's Advisory, Conciliation and Arbitration Service (ACAS) to investigate formally whether or not it should be recognized as the representative union for Laker Airways' 550 cabin staff. The TGWU is the recognized union for cabin staff on all the major British airlines that are members of the industry's National Joint Council. In 1977, the Union represented in all around 9,000 cabin staff in Britain. Laker Airways refused to go along with this argument, claiming that its Jersey registration put it outside the strict requirements of the Employment Protection Act. One reason Laker had chosen Jersey as his base was that it meant he was not forced to pay the same wages for the same grade employees as British Airways.

The TGWU had begun seeking recognition in 1976, with no success at all. In 1977 ACAS had carried out a survey of the airline's 279 cabin staff (the number then employed) and had found 108 members of the Union. Following that survey, Laker Airways had set up a staff association for its cabin staff and officially recognized it as the bargaining unit for these employees. The TGWU persisted, however, and so ACAS attempted to carry out another survey to see if there was a majority in favour of joining the TGWU and having it recognized instead. If that had happened Laker Airways would pretty soon either have had a strike on its hands or its cabin staff would have been paid as much as those on British Airways, BCal and the rest.

Laker Airways simply refused to help in any way with the survey, refusing even to distribute the survey forms. ACAS was not able to force an employer to co-operate; instead it advertised for Laker cabin staff to write in and ask for a survey form. Some 206 did so and 133 bothered to send the forms back. Of those, just 25 were found to be members of the TGWU and the Union simply faded out of the Laker Airways picture. In 1981, Laker Airways also managed to thwart a similar campaign in the United States by the Teamsters Union, as powerful in its country as the TGWU is in Britain.

Laker's view is that trade unions are needed only where there are bad employers. Of course, by his definition, his airline was not a bad employer. He is by nature a paternalistic boss. There were no set rules and no way an employee could have known when he might have been covered by Laker's benevolence, but if one of his workers was in trouble—with children, family matters, money— Laker often stepped in with aid. Such help was completely informal in nature and, as one of the leaders of the cabin staff's association said later: 'It is very difficult to work for (or fight against) a folk hero.' The staff had to put up with compulsory overtime, no pension scheme and no health plan in addition to what was already provided through the National Health Service.

Laker's most vocal opponent, of all the union leaders with whom he came into contact, was Clive Jenkins, a wily Welshman with a glib tongue and a ready, if barbed, wit. Jenkins was leading a delegation of unionists at a lengthy and tedious negotiating session with Laker while he was still at BUA. They were in Laker's office at Portland House and it was approaching early evening. 'Suddenly,' recalls Laker Airways' public relations director, Robin Flood, who was then with BUA, 'Laker noticed the time. He dragged out his overnight bag, dropped his trousers and in full view changed into his evening clothes. And then he left.' Unfortunately for Laker, his grand exit was spoiled when he couldn't remember where he was supposed to be going and had to phone Flood to find out. It coloured Jenkins's view of Laker ever afterwards.

7 · America deregulated

Just one week before Professor Alfred Kahn joined as its chairman on 10 June 1977, America's CAB had decided that the time had come to comply with the British request to give Laker his permit. Kahn had handed out heavy hints that, because he admired what Laker stood for, he would like to be involved, but the others on the Board would not wait. President Carter's choice of Kahn to head the CAB during what was to become a period of pell-mell deregulation of the airlines was an inspired one. Kahn, the head of the economics department at Cornell University, is a firm believer in more competition rather than protection. He had been involved mainly in the regulation of the energy industries with the New York State public service commission. It took two requests from the President to convince Kahn to take on the airlines, but Carter had made clear his commitment to regulatory reform—as deregulation was then called—even should a major American airline go broke. The aviation industry seemed ripe for a change in the way it was officially overseen. Kahn is a jolly man with a devastating wit that he uses to poke fun at his targets, in this case airline managements. But he got his message home, and after a couple of years of operating in a deregulated atmosphere, airline bosses, such as Eastern's Frank Borman, admitted that they had been wrong to oppose it. (There was, for example, no outcry from US airlines about deregulation, even after Braniff went bankrupt in 1982.)

Deregulation was, of course, ideally suited to Laker's free-wheeling ways. And Kahn and the rest of the American deregulators took to Laker and his ideas. They made use of the publicity that surrounded him and cheap air fares to push the virtues of deregulation. Soon after Skytrain started, Laker paid a visit to Kahn at his Washington office. The new CAB chairman said to him that he was concerned about the way the other international carriers were going after him. Laker's reply, which is tinged with irony now, was: 'Don't worry about me, Dr Kahn. I'm a survivor.'

Unlike Britain's accidental lurch in policy to adopt Laker's Skytrain, the United States' change of heart had its roots in a long and steady policy swing that had begun in the early 1970s. During the early part of the decade, and even before the 1973 OPEC oil price increase, the CAB had been bending over backwards to help the airlines because of a sharp decline in traffic. The two CAB chairmen during this period (Secor Browne, 1969–73, and Robert Timm, 1973–4) were more concerned with the airlines' troubles than with their other duty, to look after the public interest. In fact, Timm said at one point that the public interest was seeing to it that the airlines made a 12 per cent return on investment.

The CAB at various times decided that the American airlines could get together to work out how to cut their costs, regardless of the effect this might have on service to the customer. The airlines were permitted to agree on capacity cuts, for example. And they were allowed to work out how to save fuel, which sounds fine except that it was achieved by their all agreeing to fly at the same speed and thus eliminate competition that way. First under Browne and then under Timm, the CAB also implemented what was called a route moratorium. In effect, this meant ignoring requests from airlines to enter routes they were not already flying, thus protecting existing carriers. In the five years to 30 June 1969, the CAB had granted fourteen new route entries to carriers and at that date twenty-three cases were still pending. In the next five-year period to 30 June 1974, when the moratorium was in force, the CAB granted two new routes and there were forty-seven still pending at the end.

The CAB preferred to call its actions a 'policy of caution' and it was this that helped to block Laker's earlier attempts to get a permit from the American authorities for Skytrain, when it had first been approved by the British. But it was not just Skytrain that fell foul of the CAB's refusal to consider requests: no airline received permission to fly a new route. World Airways, then a supplemental (charter) operator, applied to fly a scheduled transcontinental route and was willing to use airports at each end that were not serviced by the major airlines. It was rejected.

Airlines were, however, permitted to escape from unprofitable routes. The theory justifying heavy regulation would suggest that these loss-makers should have been cross-subsidized, in the interests of the consumer, with revenues from the better routes. The CAB also let the international carriers set minimum fares for the transatlantic routes, including those for charter operators. In effect this gave IATA total freedom to fix all rates, without even government oversight of the results.

By 1974, the agency was even setting fares directly rather than accepting or rejecting those filed by carriers.

The close identification of the CAB with the wishes of the scheduled airlines became a scandal. Timm was forced to resign. There was an inevitable reaction against the abuses of over-regulation by the CAB. At the same time there were several major academic studies, including one by Kahn, questioning how much regulation was actually necessary in the airline business. The consumer movement was on the rise in the United States, led by Ralph Nader. Reducing regulation in the airline business turned into a bilateral political matter when it was adopted for different reasons by the Republican stop-gap President Gerald Ford and also by the Democratic Senator Edward Kennedy. Ford wanted to help the industry by reducing the cost of coping with regulators, while Kennedy wanted to appeal to the pro-consumer vote.

Kennedy held a series of hearings on the matter in 1974–5. His staff had cautioned him that it would be a boring and technical subject, but Kennedy decided that it might help to correct Washington's view of him as an intellectual lightweight. It turned out much better than even Kennedy can have hoped. The public's attention was grabbed, among other revelations at the hearings, by a study by one Michael Levine, an economics lecturer from Los Angeles, who had made a detailed study of the effect on air fares of California's system of regulation, which basically involved keeping fares at minimal levels. Not surprisingly, this system had resulted in air fares that were much lower than those for similar distances in the rest of the United States. Somehow, this form of regulation was turned into an example of beneficial competition. It was this same Michael Levine who later joined Kahn's CAB and became an ardent advocate of deregulation and increased competition— sometimes being privately called St Augustine for his pains.

Just in time for the presidential election in 1976, Ford came out with a policy document on international aviation. It turned out to be a feeble, conciliatory document—every little pressure group had succeeded in getting a statement included, some of them contradictory. Reducing regulation in general, and of the airlines in particular, was one of the platforms of Ford's unsuccessful presidential campaign. But the fact that there was bipartisan support for deregulating the airlines encouraged the CAB to ease its interpretation of some of the hitherto rigidly applied rules. Under the chairmanship of John Robson, who succeeded Timm and preceded Kahn, lots of speeches were made favouring more competition. Action was more limited, however, but included easing some of the restrictions on charter flights within the United States during 1976. Early in 1977, the domestic scheduled carriers were allowed to respond. First American Airlines came out with Supersaver fares, then other airlines followed with highly competitive advance purchase fares on scheduled services. This was just the sort of fare that British Airways had been trying for years to introduce on the North Atlantic. But in addition to a lack of enthusiasm from the rest of the members of IATA, it had met with total resistance from the CAB.

In its simplest form, Kahn's style of deregulation can be defined as encouraging as many airlines to fly on as many routes as possible, with fares as low as possible. Long before the law had been changed to help him (that happened in 1978), the CAB began to go all out to push this policy. Kahn always wanted to be challenged in the courts. The case would likely have ended up in the Court of Appeals in Washington DC, a court Kahn reckons was susceptible to economic arguments. He had managed to obtain agreement from the rest of the Board that if it came to a legal challenge, he would be allowed to plead his own case and not be obliged to rely on the CAB's lawyers. The Kahn Board had the clear backing of the President. During John Robson's last weeks at the CAB, Carter had tried to spell out in a letter the new administration's policy of encouraging more competition, especially on international routes. For Kahn, Carter's words became a battle cry. In a letter to Kahn on 6 October 1977, the President said:

We should seek international aviation agreements that permit low-fare innovations in scheduled services, expanded and liberalized charter operations, nonstop international service, and competition among multiple US carriers in markets of sufficient size. We should also avoid government restrictions on airline capacity.

Without wishing to belittle him, it can be said that airline deregulation turned out to be President Carter's one clearcut success during his four-year term at the White House.

The letter indirectly revealed the items in the Bermuda 2 Agreement with Britain that so irked the Americans, once they had woken up to just what they had signed. They were also particularly upset that charters were not dealt with at the same time as scheduled services in the Bermuda 2 negotiations. The memorandum of understanding on charters between the two countries had expired right in the middle of the main talks, and the British persuaded the Americans that the memorandum should be extended. Part of this deal was that advance booking charters (ABCs) were to be allowed from 1 April 1977, with the advance booking period reduced to 'only' 45 days. It took some time for the remainder of the charter deal to be settled after the Bermuda 2 treaty had been finalized, and the outcome was more restrictive than the Americans had hoped. Alan Boyd had lamely explained to the House of Representatives that the US delegation had decided not to make a charter agreement a precondition to an agreement on scheduled services with the British because charters accounted for only a quarter of the market. Kahn was later scathing about the 'narrowness of this analysis, which ignored the dynamics of the marketplace'.

There was a genuine quandary in the United States over charters, which were operators that had spurred low-fare competition from the scheduled carriers in the first place. A large number of these supplemental carriers (charter operators) were now beginning to get into trouble. Their original source of business (troop-carrying in the Vietnam war) had dried up—they were among America's economic victims of peace. Within the United States the rules had been changed and their low fares were being attacked by the scheduled carriers. And now, thanks to the scheduled carriers' response to Laker's Skytrain, they were about to be attacked on the North Atlantic, too. In 1977, the American

Justice Department, the keeper of America's business morals, had made no bones about its fears should the charter operators go under.

> If charters to Great Britain lose their economic viability [as a result of the IATA pricing proposals], so do the charter carriers themselves. And if the charter carriers go out of business, regulatory and political resistance of foreign governments to the concept of a freely competitive charter market would make attempted re-entry a long, costly, and probably futile exercise. . . . The scheduled carriers would be free to eliminate these discounts without fear of the re-emergence of a competitive check.

Just after he arrived as the chairman of the CAB, and just before the signing of the Bermuda 2 Agreement with Britain, Kahn admits that he was 'importuned' by the supplementals to intercede on their behalf. He made some telephone calls, but decided at this late stage that he was too ill-informed to become involved.

There was an odd conflict for Kahn, and the rest of those at the CAB interested in increasing competition, that arose out of the three fares that the IATA carriers had cooked up, ostensibly to compete with Laker's Skytrain. There was no concern about the Standby fare, which was directly comparable with Laker's instant-booking, walk-on service. But Budget and APEX were not new inventions; they had been emerging for some time in various forms. The target of these fares was the charter trade, which the scheduled carriers had become involved in as heavily as any of the charter operators. Budget fares were approved by the CAB with some reluctance, but Super APEX was turned down, a decision reversed by the White House. Kahn was convinced that if there was no parallel freeing of conditions applying to the charter operators, or if there should be any subsequent tightening of charter rules, then as a result 'lower fares like British Airways Super APEX fare would have to be withdrawn,' he explained, with or without Laker on the North Atlantic market.

Kahn's CAB had almost as much difficulty in selecting which American carriers should be allowed to pick up the new routes that were being opened up. All the carriers, however much it went against their normal inclination, pretended to be in favour of low fares. If low fares were what the CAB now wanted, then that is what it got, with a vengeance, in all the airlines' applications. The dilemma is well illustrated by the Dallas–Fort Worth to London route opened up by Bermuda 2. Pan Am wanted it, but the CAB would have done almost anything rather than concede that. Braniff wanted it, too, and had the practical advantage of serving the Texas region and therefore having an existing traffic 'feed' for the international route. As Mike Levine put it in an internal CAB memorandum: 'It is troubling to us that we have a carrier like Braniff presenting itself as a low-fare carrier on the North Atlantic (where it is seeking entry) in sharp contrast to its high-fare monopolistic behaviour in South America where it faces non-competitive conditions.' Most South American nations simply refuse to allow any competition on routes to their countries; it is a region where the IATA cartel firmly rules. For Dallas–London, the CAB eventually chose Braniff as the lesser of two evils.

Much the most important development favouring international deregulation on the North Atlantic during the 1977–8 period was not Laker or Bermuda 2 but the more liberal bilateral agreements that Kahn's team bullied out of Belgium and the Netherlands. Kahn was so disgusted with the Bermuda 2 Agreement and the way the British were operating it that he said he 'was going to stick it to the British'. By this he meant that he was going to try to arrange an end run around Britain and thus arrange other air services and low fares so that passengers would be attracted away from Britain to other Continental airports (e.g. Brussels and Amsterdam). Up to this time, around two-thirds of all passengers on the North Atlantic went to Europe via London's Heathrow Airport.

Kahn's view was confirmed just seven months after Bermuda 2 was signed when the British manipulated the treaty's terms to block the low fares that Braniff had proposed for its Dallas–London service. The inaugural flight with guests had taken place, but the British blocked the start of paying scheduled services. There were those in the Executive and Congress who agitated for the Americans to renounce Bermuda 2 an unlikely event, but it showed the depth of feeling that was aroused in Washington. The British were not really objecting to Braniff's fares as such, but to the special fares the airline had introduced on what are called beyond points—in this case other airports in America's south-western states. They were low enough, the British feared, to siphon off potential traffic from BCal's new service to Houston. In the end, both sides saved face. The Americans made threats and Braniff retained, more or less, its original low fares on Dallas–London, while the British blocked the lowest of its fares from other points.

Belgium and the Netherlands are small countries with small amounts of passenger traffic arising within their own borders. The two countries' national airlines, respectively Sabena and KLM, rely on attracting passengers from neighbouring countries by various means. In the pre-deregulation period, occasionally this was done by lower fares tied to strict conditions, but more often by hidden rebates or higher commissions paid to travel agents. Both countries were ready-made for an attack by Kahn's team. In return for allowing their airlines to fly to more points in the United States, the CAB persuaded them to accept 'country-of-origin rules' on matters such as fares. These rules meant that whatever the American authorities approved as the fare for carriers operating between, say, New York and Amsterdam, the Dutch had to accept. And vice versa.

These bilateral agreements led in turn to the British being less restrictive in their interpretation of the Bermuda 2 rules. Much more important still, they also led to West Germany and its state airline, Lufthansa, agreeing to a competitive bilateral agreement with the United States. Quite out of character, but pressured by the potential loss of Lufthansa's traffic to KLM (Düsseldorf is only an hour or so's drive from Amsterdam), in November 1978 the Germans caved in: country-of-origin rules were accepted. A common feature of all these new agreements, including Bermuda 2, was a large increase in the number of American carriers allowed to fly. And apart from the treaty with the British, the other agreements had no control on capacity. The only thing that the Continentals refused the Americans was what is called double disapproval. Agreeing to this would have meant that only if the regulators of both countries involved, say, West Germany and the United States, disapproved of a fare could the carrier that wanted to introduce it be prevented from doing so. Unthinkably for the Germans, that would have given the Americans some control over what Lufthansa did in its own country—a denting of the principle of sovereignty.

Achieving changes in both low fares and routes, by increasing the number of gateways and the number of carriers allowed to fly, was the key, Kahn felt. Easing the rules of entry into a market was a structural precondition of permanent change, he says; 'otherwise all we would have had was a short burst of low-fare traffic and it would all have returned to the way it had been.' Kahn was not concerned with the nationality of the new carriers being allowed to fly—American or foreign. He did not care where they came from as long as they were present on a route. Kahn characterized what he was doing as 'trading liberalization for liberalization', though some in the American aviation establishment feared that giving away all those gateways in the American hinterland was like giving away several geese that laid golden eggs. Allowing foreign carriers access to the traffic at these gateways reduced the domestic carriers' main marketing advantage. At one point the CAB feared that it might have let the carriers move too fast on low fares alone. But at least for charter flights, securing country-of-origin rules (which are set by the country in which the passengers originate regardless of the nationality of the airline) sustained the competitive threat to the established carriers.

Sad to say, for Laker and Laker fans his airline's presence on the London–New York market was a bonus, not a precursor to these structural changes. His presence did, however, speed the rate of change that occurred through the publicity that he generated about low fares. Kahn is an avowed Laker admirer and so is reluctant to say it too loudly, but Laker and his Skytrain were only of use as propaganda for deregulation and low fares. 'Skytrain dramatized the effects of deregulation,' says Kahn. Laker himself is a natural publicity seeker.

8 · Freddie and the press

In the nicest possible way, Laker took advantage of the press. It was there to be used. He paid his dues by providing more or less guaranteed stories with juicy quotes and usable pictures. He also had a way with most journalists. Right from the start, he learned that it paid off to take the press on a field trip so that they could see at first hand what was going on. Back in 1953, for instance, when he wanted to promote the virtues of an aircraft called the Tudor to which his company had made many technical improvements, he took a party of journalists to Hamburg. Later, when he was head of BUA, he took some journalists on a publicity trip of the VC-10 jet to Africa, though here he was aiming mainly at local publicity to generate traffic. The VC-10 had a cargo door and so, to demonstrate its usefulness, he arranged to borrow Rolls-Royce's demonstrator Silver Cloud. This was loaded in and out at every stop and used to ferry local dignatories to receptions and parties. To dress things up still further—and to guarantee even better pictures—he also persuaded Courtaulds to pay for some models to give fashion shows along the way.

Another finishing touch was that Laker insisted that the Rolls' registration number be changed from the traditional Rolls-Royce number of 100 LG to RR1. It caused immense amounts of paperwork—and string pulling—with the Customs in each country the tour visited.

The publicity about the Africa trip paid off in a very profitable way for BUA. It helped Laker win for that airline some scheduled routes to South America that had been operated by BOAC. The state-owned airline had asked for a four-year subsidy to run what were, for it, loss-making routes. The Conservative Government was very unhappy at the prospect of paying a subsidy and had just had thrust before it the example of a private enterprise carrier that was willing to take on the routes as they stood. No sooner had BUA been temporarily granted the routes than the Tories lost a general election and the Labour Party was back in power. By starting the routes speedily, and gathering another round of publicity, Laker defused a Labour Party pre-election promise that a Labour Government would 'in no way be bound by this hurried and questionable deal'. The temporary licence was turned into a permanent one.

There has long been a special relationship between Laker and the pro-free enterprise Beaverbook newspapers, notably the *Daily Express*. Its story about BUA's South American routes was splashed across the front page, headlined 'Rolling down to Rio'. When Laker had the use of car ferries across the English Channel on a 'Fly British' theme, the *Express* covered the story. It supported Laker to the hilt when, during the period that he was being denied by one government or another the right to fly Skytrain, publicity was his only weapon.

Laker at one point claimed that he could make Concorde pay even if British Airways could not. In 1974, the state-owned airline was trying to evade responsibility for the supersonic loss-maker. It had submitted a memorandum pointing out that operating the aircraft, even without having to pay any contribution towards its initial development cost, was going to cost it at least £20 million a year. Nobody took Laker's claim seriously—he was called 'the cheeky chappie of British aviation' by one paper—but his claim caught the headlines, especially in the *Daily Express*. It took the heat off Concorde. Within a week or so, BA had changed its tune, under political pressure from the Government. And later, Laker was able to claim that he had 'saved' Concorde.

Laker learned to speak in headlines and would do whatever was necessary to get into the newspapers or on television. He was not averse to editing his own remarks as time went by, to make them more catchy. His statement immediately after Peter Shore had tried to prevent Skytrain from ever getting into service had been 'Skytrain will be on the books until the day I die.' First for radio audiences and later for everybody else, it became the better-known and remembered: 'Skytrain will remain on my planes until the day I die.' He would leap into action as soon as a camera was ready, adopting any pose that was asked of him. At one press gathering his mother produced a present for her son, a pair of gaudy Woolworth underpants.

Having obtained permission to fly Skytrain, Laker was rarely out of the papers, usually with champagne in hand, always with a big happy grin. He would wave his arms in the air, play at being an aircraft, stick his thumb up or clench his fists triumphantly above his head. Once, in an elaborate spoof, he appeared at a party on stage complete with Laker Airways hostess hat and flight bag, wearing a newspaper placard around his neck proclaiming: 'I'm Freddie, fly me'. It has become the most overworked Lakerism of all, but it was not original. It was a copy of a sexist advertisement by National Airlines that showed its stewardesses in a suggestive extension of that old airways line: 'Coffee, tea, or me?'

Skytrain in 1977–8 created a whole new industry for journalists, writing about low air fares on the North Atlantic. Laker would help them by producing, even before asked, the exact number of passengers carried up to the previous day's flight and the operating profit made to that date. As long as he was dealing with the aviation or travel press, Laker knew just what he was doing. At the end, however, when the story had passed into the hands of financial and business journalists, Laker found that his charm was insufficient to divert awkward questions. Then Laker went to ground.

9 · Overexpansion

On 26 September 1977 the first Skytrain took off from Gatwick for New York. 'It's the best show in town,' said Laker, but the combination of frenetic publicity about Skytrain and the availability of some rival cheap seats on the scheduled carriers kept his passenger load to manageable proportions. The flight from London to New York had 73 of its 345 seats empty—and the passengers included scores of journalists and television people anxious to cover the event, even though (rare for an aviation inaugural flight) Laker made them pay their own fares, £59 one way, £64 the other. The return flight from New York, swelled by American journalists plus some of those from Britain coming straight back, was almost full.

By the time the Skytrain service began, most of the conditions that had once been attached to it in London had been negotiated away. Laker Airways was still not allowed to start selling tickets for the day's flight before 4 a.m. that morning. But it was allowed to sell the tickets either at Gatwick Airport, to where its operation had been switched from Stansted as part of Britain's help-Gatwick Airport policy, or at a converted tobacconist shop at London's Victoria Station. The shop had been deserted for some time and Laker simply stripped it, put a sign over the doorway and installed a partition at the back with a couple of sales windows. Dotted around the open space in front were some simple shelves for people to fill out the form needed to buy a ticket. Total sales staff there and at Gatwick came to six or seven people who had to keep a tally on how many tickets had been sold at each end to avoid overbooking. There was a full load out of London on the first Sunday after Skytrain began, but since such loads were not too common at first, even this simple sales task was not onerous.

The New York operation was more elaborate, but still much less lavish than that of most airlines. Even though it had a permit from the US Government to operate from New York's Kennedy Airport, the upstart airline had been told it could not set up shop and sell tickets at the Airport itself. Unlike the European system, where a national authority owns and operates virtually all major airports, in the United States individual carriers either own or take out long-term leases on their terminal space and gates. Every time Laker Airways thought that it had a deal, it fell through. One of the obstacles was the New York Port Authority, which did not like the idea of queues of long-haired hippies camping in the tidy airport terminal buildings in its jurisdiction while they waited for a chance to buy a Skytrain ticket. Ticket sales would have to be 'off Airport'. So early in September, Laker Airways' manager in New York began cruising in his car around the streets of New York between Manhattan and Kennedy. His persistence was rewarded in Queens. Close to the Van Wyck Expressway—the route to Kennedy Airport—and to a subway station, he spotted a new building with an empty ground floor. After a rapid consultation with the building's architects, Laker himself turned up on a Sunday morning two weeks before Skytrain's launch, looked at the building and shook hands on a 21-year lease. Laker's style of instant management and the Americans' way of conducting business deals often matched in this fashion. Now that Skytrain had a place where queues could be isolated and passengers sold their tickets and checked in, United Air Lines gave Laker houseroom in its terminal.

Laker Airways mounted the cheapest sales operation in the history of modern scheduled aviation services. Laker accepted either cash or a Visa credit card on which, at that time, the airline was paying the banks a 2·5 per cent service fee. There were no bad debts, since the Visa-issuing banks accepted that risk on behalf of merchants accepting the card. In later times, Laker had to increase the amount of advertising needed to support Skytrain, but in these early days the newspapers and television stations did almost all of it for him. All that was needed was a few advertisements giving the telephone number for a recorded information service plus the times of the flights and where and when the booking offices were open. During the first financial year that Skytrain was operating, to

March 1979, which therefore included the first six months of the Los Angeles Skytrain as well, the total cost of ticketing, sales and promotion for the whole of Laker Airways (including holidays and European charter flights) came to 4·7 per cent of its total operating expenses. By comparison, the same percentage for British Airways that year was 19 per cent and for British Caledonian 13 per cent, and the average for the members of IATA was around 15 per cent.

Until the other airlines came out with their rival Standby, Budget and APEX fares—all with strictly controlled capacity at these low prices—the standard economy ticket between London and New York had been £196. It included a meal of sorts, though passengers had to pay cartelized prices for drinks and for a headset. Laker's version was strictly no frills: first come, first served, queue all night if necessary, and everything was charged for, including meals. But on Skytrain you could bring your own food (anything, fish and chips included) if you wished.

Laker's fleet in the summer of 1978 consisted of two old Boeing 707s and four BAC 1–11s, and he now had no fewer than four DC-10s, all of the short-range type designed for use within the United States. The first two, purchased through Mitsui, had been delivered way back in 1972, when he had first thought he was going to get the licence for Skytrain. The third, delivered in January 1974, was also one of Mitsui's aircraft that had been ordered for All-Nippon Airways. It had been parked for some time in the corrosion-free desert atmosphere of Arizona. The Japanese trading company was glad to be rid of it and terms were even better than those for the first two: 6 per cent over ten years and all to be repaid out of revenue. The fourth DC-10, contracted for in July 1976, was bought by Laker with his usual eye to the main chance. It was McDonnell Douglas's second-ever DC-10 (known as Ship No. 2) and it had been used heavily in the flight test and certification programme. Its price and terms reflected this, though Laker preferred to say only that it was 'slightly used'. Finance for this was arranged through the Clydesdale Bank.

The Skytrain service to New York was just four months old when Laker went a-buying again, this time for two more short-range DC-10s. The deal was organized by the Japanese Government under what became known as the Samurai loan programme. Japan's trade surplus with the United States had reached embarrassingly large proportions, so the Japanese Government advanced loans to major Japanese trading companies that enabled them to buy, for example, aircraft from the US. This reduced the trade surplus. The aircraft could then be leased out (the trading companies themselves had no direct use for them) and Laker cashed in. Effectively, Mitsui financed his fifth and sixth DC-10s at 8·25 per cent interest over twenty years, with no down payment—favourable terms indeed.

Having beaten the British Government in court and then having been adopted on the London–New York route as part of the Bermuda 2 settlement, it was more or less a foregone conclusion that Laker's Skytrain would add the London–Los Angeles designation at some point. Unless, that is, the New York Skytrain immediately failed. It didn't: Laker proudly claimed profits from the first week. British aviation officials feared that BCal would simply fail again on the Los Angeles route, as it had the first time. So, on 5 May 1978, the CAA granted Laker this second scheduled right and this time the Americans promptly responded.

Laker could do no wrong in Washington during this period, with Professor Alfred Kahn at the helm of the CAB. Laker could do no wrong anywhere else, it seemed. In the Queen's Birthday Honours in June 1978, under the auspices of the Callaghan Government that he had soundly beaten in the courts, he was knighted for his services to aviation. He was on the up and up and in friendly mood, even towards politicians. 'They seem to have said: "It was a fair fight and he has won." I think that the Government must have now accepted that competition is the name of the game.' While confessing what everybody knew, that he considered politicians were dreadful people, Laker thought that his knighthood seemed to show that perhaps they really could be honourable at least some of the time.

With his knighthood and his second designation for a scheduled service across the North Atlantic in his pocket, just before the first anniversary of the New York Skytrain and the launch of the second one to Los Angeles, Sir Freddie dropped a bombshell on a dumbfounded aviation business. He already had more than enough aircraft to cope, but he announced that he planned to spend £380 million to buy no less than fifteen more widebodied jets. There were to be five of the long-range DC-10-30s and ten of the European Airbuses. When he received the Los Angeles licence he had idly dropped a hint that he was considering buying two Boeing

747 jumbos but that had correctly been dismissed as a Lakerism. This time he was serious. He also revealed that he was hoping to use some of this fleet to start a round-the-world Skytrain that instantly became known as Globetrain. It would need licences to fly between London and Hong Kong and from there to Los Angeles in order to hook up with his existing route licence. (Pan Am is still the only airline to operate such a route.) At this stage, the Airbuses were said to be needed for Laker's package holiday routes in Europe.

There was an ominously perceptive headline in *The Times* the day after the stories had been digested. It asked: 'Where will Sir Freddie get the cash?' The company's net worth in the year to March 1977 (the latest published accounts then available to *The Times*) was £3·8 million and net borrowings were £23 million, though the existing aircraft and spares were undervalued in the books by £22 million. Profits were a slim £776,000, though this was more than wiped out by a £1.2 million exchange loss. But since these accounts had been prepared, Laker had taken on another two DC-10s through the Samurai-financed deal, however advantageous that may have seemed.

There had been inevitable objections to Laker Airways' receiving the London–Los Angeles designation, notably from BCal, which still held a licence. It had served the route from March 1973 to November 1974 and had then pulled out as part of its survival plan to cut mounting losses. By late 1974, BCal had built up about a 12 per cent share of the Los Angeles–London passenger traffic, against British Airways' 16 per cent; the rest was split between TWA and Pan Am, until the latter pulled off the route in May 1975 when it, too, was retrenching. As part of its effort to prevent Laker getting the Los Angeles designation from the CAA, BCal joined what had become the fashionable trend and offered low fares, which must have hurt. This bid was disallowed by the CAA, however, since BCal was limiting the lowest fares to just a handful of seats on each flight. The Skytrain fare was £84 to Los Angeles and $220 to London in the low season and £96 out and $248 back in the summer peak. The standard economy ticket at that time was £539–£614 return, depending on the season, with comparable APEX rates of £235 and £312.

The slowness of Laker's start in this Californian market was, therefore, a surprise. It took Laker Airways over a year to reach break-even on the Los Angeles run, losing more than £5 million between the start-up and early 1980. The average load factor was no better than 32 per cent for months at a time. And the losses more than offset the profits being made from the New York Skytrain, which Laker reckoned to be £2 million in its first twelve months of operation (to September 1978).

There were several reasons for the disappointing Los Angeles operation. First, Laker Airways' existing, short-range DC-10s simply could not make the trip from London to Los Angeles in one leg and had to stop for fuel. They also often had to stop for fuel at Prestwick on the way back to London if the prevailing winds were unkind. A virtue was made of necessity; by stopping at Bangor, in Maine, the passengers cleared American Customs in a relatively civilized manner, rather than fighting Los Angeles International Airport, which is one of the world's worst. But the additional two and a half hours on the journey time did not appeal to the southern Californian market. On many occasions, Laker Airways accepted that it was not going to win people over to a stopping Skytrain. To cut costs, when the joint loads of a particular day's New York and Los Angeles runs were less than would fill one aircraft, these flights were consolidated. In this event, the Los Angeles passengers had to clear customs at Kennedy, New York, which is only marginally better than Los Angeles. This situation was not resolved until December 1979, when Laker took delivery of the first of the five long-range DC-10-30s that were part of the 1978 maxi-order.

Another problem for Skytrain was that Californians were, at first, put off by the heavily publicized (though largely incorrect) image of an aircraft filled with unwashed, back-packing students. This was in part a hangover from the publicity surrounding the New York Skytrain at the end of the summer in 1978, when what became known as Lakerville emerged at London's Victoria Station. It was only in small measure a Laker-created problem. The established carriers had sold Standby tickets to American students wanting to visit Europe and they had left the USA over a staggered period as their studies finished. But they all wanted to return home at the same time, at the end of September. The scheduled carriers, facing higher levels of demand from ordinary full-fare paying passengers, did not have the capacity or the willingness to cope with the surge of Standby passengers. So these passengers turned to Laker Airways, which already faced the same problem with the Skytrainers it had brought over.

The students camped in long queues for days as they waited for a chance to get on a flight. All the cheap seats could only be sold on the day of departure. The weather was awful and conditions became very insanitary. Some enterprising passengers began to keep lists of people's names in order of their arrival, thus allowing them to take some time out of the queue. With the use of computers to keep the list of names, this was the formal system the American and British authorities finally agreed on in early 1979 as the best way to eliminate the problem in the future. This was called the rollover system; it allowed people to put their names down for the next flight once that day's had been filled. In a moment of rare common sense, the CAA and CAB decided that it would not breach Skytrain's rules too obviously. It did, however, mark another significant step in changing Laker's original walk-on, no-frills Skytrain into a conventional scheduled service.

There is a third possible reason why Skytrain took so long to become profitable on the Los Angeles route, and it concerns the response of the established carriers. As they had before, at the start of the New York route, BA and TWA anticipated Skytrain's start-up and introduced rival low fares even before Laker's first flight. This immediate, or even anticipatory, fare matching was a new departure for the scheduled carriers and is now standard practice.

By early 1979, Laker was stuck with massive overcapacity. In February and March of that year, his fifth and sixth DC-10s were delivered. He pushed forward with plans to fly many other routes. In addition to his plans for Hong Kong and a round-the-world service, he had long wanted to fly to Australia. Back in 1969, he had applied to the Australian Department of Civil Aviation for a licence to operate charter flights there. That failed to pass the first test, since BOAC (when it was still a separate corporation) and the Australian national carrier, Qantas, both claimed heavy losses on services from Britain to Australia because of existing charter operators. This rebuff, and many more that followed, did not stop Laker from trying to persuade the British and Australian authorities to allow him to offer low-fare services between the two countries. Apart from a handful of *ad hoc* charters in the intervening years, usually for another tour operator, he had not flown to Australia since his earliest days in the 1950s with government troop-carrying flights.

Laker Airways, and other carriers like Singapore International Airlines, fell foul of a policy of the Australian Government, devised in cahoots with the British Government, that became known as ICAP, or (Australia's) International Civil Aviation Policy. Under this, the two flag carriers Qantas and BA sought to cut out competition for all traffic that was to be carried from one end to the other of the so-called Kangaroo route.

This policy was heavily influenced by Charles Halton, head civil servant in Australia's Department of Civil Aviation, an ex-British official who worked for a time with the Canadian railways and then moved on to join the Australian transport authorities. Like Britain's George Rogers, he likes matters to be bureaucratically tidy. In this case, the policy set out to share the traffic more or less equally between Qantas and BA, with no irrelevant competitors (i.e., Skytrain or anybody else) getting in the way.

The most blatant example of what this meant in practice concerns not Laker's unsuccessful efforts to get into the market, but those of Singapore Airlines (SIA). It had managed to carve out about a one-third share of the Australian–British market by offering low fares, almost no-cost stopovers in Singapore on the way, excellent service and heavy advertising using enticing Oriental stewardesses. For Singapore, a small country, it not only meant a fast-growing and profitable airline, and all the employment that brought, but also large amounts of foreign currency from travellers as they spent two or three days in Singapore that they otherwise would not have done. ICAP at first proposed banning the stopovers altogether. After intense political pressure the rules were softened, but not much. SIA was cut back from carrying 4,000 passengers a week on this route to a maximum of 350 and had to introduce a significant charge for a stopover along the way.

What chance did Laker have in such an environment? The chairman of Qantas at the time, Sir Lenox Hewitt, says: 'I always regarded Freddie as a great huckster.' There was little love lost between the two through the newspaper columns; the two met infrequently and then only in Washington DC. Sir Lenox made sure that the inconsistencies in Laker's pitch to get into Australia did not go unnoticed. The number of people that were expected to be carried—and, more important to the Australian Government, how many of them were to be Australians taking currency out or foreigners bringing currency in—varied over time. Sometimes it would be said by Laker that half would be Australians and at others, one-third. The total numbers involved changed, too.

But the most damaging thing for Laker's chances were his conflicting statements to the Australian House of Representatives Select Committee on tourism and to Britain's CAA. In 1977, he told the Australian committee that his proposed charter service would bring more British tourists to Australia than take Australians out. In his application to the CAA in London in September of that year, he described how it would be quite the opposite. Drawing on his North Atlantic experience with advance booking charters, Laker explained that through marketing efforts, his airline had swung from 'nil foreign originating traffic ... to where we now carry more USA and Canadian originating passengers than UK originating. This,' he said for British ears, 'is an exercise we wish to repeat with Australia.' The Australian *Financial Review* headlined its piece: 'Laker's bob-each-way in cheap flights quest'.

It would have taken a great deal less marketing effort to win over the Australian public. They were anxious to have low-cost travel back to mother countries in Europe. It was the Australians who were the second biggest group of contributors to the 'Save Freddie Fund' after the bankruptcy, even though he had never operated there. There has been a great deal of mudslinging about whether Laker would have offered cheaper fares than the establishment carriers, but that did not confuse the general public at all. They were well aware that Qantas and BA offered cheap fares, but in limited quantities and with strict and lengthy advance booking periods. It remains standard practice in Australia to have to book ahead six months or more for a holiday visit along the Kangaroo route to be sure of getting a seat at all.

Laker had applied to the British authorities for a licence to operate Skytrain to Australia in 1981, but he had been turned down by the CAA which, by now, was concerned about his financial position. Laker Airways had appealed against this rejection to the Secretary of State for Trade, John Biffen, but that appeal lapsed when the airline went broke. He had never formally applied for a licence at the Australian end because, he felt, there was no point until he had one from his own country's authorities. If the British had ever allowed it, Laker always believed that he could at least get a licence to fly to Perth in Western Australia, if nowhere else. The director of tourism there, Noel Semmons, was an avid Laker fan. Without a feed of traffic from the rest of the country, however, that route would have been impossibly thin and therefore unprofitable. In order not to offend people, though, the reason given for not trying was that Laker did not want to gain entry by the back door.

An even more important challenge had been Laker's attempt to get his airline into Hong Kong, and from there on round the world. By the middle of 1979, Laker Airways had licences from London, Manchester and Prestwick to Los Angeles, Honolulu, Tokyo and Sharja (UAE). Under the terms of Bermuda 2 and its later amendments, the American authorities would, Laker believed, allow him to hook up those routes. All that was missing was the right to fly London–Hong Kong which, as a Crown Colony, was covered by some very odd legislation indeed.

For years BA had a monopoly on the London–Hong Kong route and was exempt from having to apply for a licence to serve it. The Hong Kong Government had grown increasingly dissatisfied with BA's service and in 1980 applications for the route were made to the Colony's Air Transport Licensing Authority (ATLA) by BCal, Cathay Pacific, a Hong Kong-based airline owned mainly by the Swire group, and Laker Airways. BCal and Cathay Pacific were approved, but Laker was turned down. On top of BA's existing seven flights a week with Boeing 747s, Cathay was told it could operate three 747 flights a week and BCal seven DC-10 flights a week. BCal ordered two DC-10s as a result. In March 1980 the CAA too turned Laker down and did not accept ATLA's judgement on Cathay Pacific. Because British legislation requires the CAA to favour British-based carriers, the authority rejected the idea that Cathay Pacific should be allowed to fly to London. The CAA's judgment was quite specific about Laker.

> Although at present capacity on the London–Hong Kong route does not fully meet demand, all the parties other than Laker argued—and the CAA agrees—that demand is by no means unlimited.... further traffic stimulation through low fares is likely to be limited insofar as a significant proportion of past growth is already attributable to the low fares that have been introduced in recent years; that particular orange is unlikely to hold an endless supply of juice.

Laker's success on the North Atlantic, the CAA argued firmly, was due to the transfer of charter passengers to low fares of one sort or another on established scheduled carriers as well as to Laker's Skytrain. There was no sizeable reservoir of existing charter business on the London–Hong Kong route available to be transferred. 'Behind the CAA's concern,' explains Ray Colegate, who is head of the CAA's Economic Services Group, 'was that Laker should be able to take on any additional routes within his existing fleet of DC-10s.' It was not spelled out in any of the CAA decisions during this period, including in the Hong Kong case, but there were beginning to be official worries about just how stretched Laker's balance sheet was becoming.

The Hong Kong Government was outraged that its local carrier Cathay Pacific had been rejected. Specifically for the route to London, it had purchased Rolls-Royce-powered Boeing 747s to join its Rolls-Royce-powered TriStars, the mainstay of its fleet. Government officials from the colony asked the Secretary of State at the time, John Nott, to give a political direction under the Civil Aviation Act to the CAA. With the Peter Shore case in mind, Nott refused, turning instead to the normal quasi-judicial authority he had under the Act, in this case the interests of aiding a dependent territory. Cathay was in, but Nott, who is a right-wing Tory inclined to encourage competition in any circumstances, approved Laker's appeal, too. He rejected the CAA's arguments that there was insufficient traffic on the route to support all four carriers. This was the first time that a CAA decision had been reversed by government since it had been established in 1971. Nott even rejected the CAA's rejection of Laker's case concerning the forgotten man. 'That rankled, especially when he said that the CAA had taken too short-term a view,' Colegate said later. There was a feeling around Whitehall at the time that Nott had climbed on the Laker bandwaggon, which was a very 'in' thing for Tories to do, the more so since Laker was a hero of Prime Minister Margaret Thatcher.

The matter then returned to the Hong Kong authority, ATLA. Its reaction was predictable. Cathay Pacific was approved and so was BCal, but Laker Airways was rejected. Adding a Skytrain service, said ATLA's panel of lay members, would put an intolerable financial strain on the other three airlines. BCal's chairman, Adam Thomson, now that he was on the good side of the decision, called the lay panel courageous for 'letting common sense prevail'. What he would have said if BCal had been rejected but not Cathay Pacific is anyone's guess.

The antique legislation that covers civil aviation in Hong Kong still refers to Britain's having two airline corporations (BOAC and BEA). It also allows no appeals against decisions and has no mechanism to allow the Secretary of State back in London—still the overriding authority on aviation in the Colony—to give ATLA a direction in the way he can to the CAA. Laker asked the British Government to persuade Hong Kong's Governor to grant Laker Airways exempt status, alongside BA, while the legislation was being brought up to date. While the first part of his request was turned down, the British Government was trying to work out how to modify the Colony's aviation law when Laker went bust. That effort, too, seems to have died with Skytrain.

These rejections left Laker with sizeable overcapacity. He now had eleven DC-10s to fill. So, in 1979 when the pound was growing stronger against the dollar thanks to North Sea oil, he turned to the idea of charters to Florida. More accurately, the original idea for this came from Harry Goodman of a rival tour operator, Intasun. Spain had been the primary destination for sun-seeking Britons for years, but Spanish costs had begun to rise sharply, partly as a result of the political changes in that country. British tour companies were finding Spain hard to sell. So why not go to some other source of sun, where costs might be lower? Miami and its surroundings are used by Americans mainly in the winter, when it turns into a suburb of New York. In the summer the hotels are half empty and vulnerable to a block deal. Harry Goodman's problem was finding some airline operator to carry his passengers. So he teamed up with Laker and, to a lesser extent, the American carrier Air Florida, which had grown mightily on the back of deregulation.

It did not take Laker long to realize that he could turn this subcontract to his own advantage. There was a change in the designation for the London–Miami route, which was due to take effect in March 1980, when an amendment to Bermuda 2 allowed two carriers from each side to fly. Laker applied for and was granted the route. 'It was,' said Ray Colegate, 'one of the more blatant pieces of transformation ever seen in air licensing.' Goodman immediately switched his Intasun business to Air Florida, though Laker did well during the ensuing eighteen months, carrying tours from his own holiday companies and from others who joined the rush to Miami, such as Cosmos.

At one time Laker considered operating to Boston and Philadelphia, though these plans never came to anything. But he did apply for a designation to operate London–Tampa, which had been added to the list of gateways between Britain and the United States by the broadened Bermuda 2½, as it was now known. Laker was the only British applicant and so got the route by default. Tampa is close to Florida's gold coast and was supposed to turn into a superb holiday route, at least while the pound stayed strong. That it did not helped to bring Laker down. Sterling's decline and the subsequent drop in British traffic to Florida also hurt other carriers. Air Florida says that about half of its mounting operating losses in the latter part of 1981 were due to the deterioration of European currencies against the dollar.

From the time in 1978 that Laker announced he was going to order Airbuses, he had planned to fly to Europe, and on scheduled routes, not just inclusive tours. Fares within Europe are notoriously high. The aviation business there is organized to favour the national carriers, and the fares are cartelized through IATA. The airlines also operate largely under what are known as pooling arrangements. Since there is typically just one carrier from each country operating on a particular route, the two work within a formula that tends to equalize profits, regardless of which carrier actually flies the most passengers. The theory is that this is better for the public since it smooths out schedules. In practice it means that the carrier does not have to try too hard since there is no choice open to the customer. One result is much higher air fares than within the United States, but also (a much more telling example) an average of 20 per cent higher than the Middle East. Fares between EEC countries average 50–100 per cent higher than the airlines' operating costs.

In theory, all this cartelization is against the provisions of the Treaty of Rome that established the bones of the European Economic Community. In a different form, Article 85 of the Rome Treaty provides the EEC with just as tough rules favouring competition and banning anti-trust activities as has the United States. There have even been court verdicts upholding the view that what is done in civil aviation in the EEC, in the name of the member governments, is in clear breach of the Rome Treaty. The

British Government under Margaret Thatcher has sided with the view that there should be more competition in aviation, though only in a half-hearted way when compared with what happened in America under President Carter. Nevertheless, it all provided fertile ground for Laker's imagination to till. The trouble has been, however, that theory is simply unable to do much about the practical politics of civil aviation in the EEC.

In his more rational moments, Laker accepted that he did not stand much chance of getting even a few routes into Europe. The Government wants to change things slowly, he said: 'they want policy to evolve. But,' he went on, 'trying to do it politically means they won't do anything and it'll come to nothing, like everything else done politically. I want to get a can-opener on Europe . . . but it's taken me thirty years to get to America. I'll be dead before I get a Skytrain into Europe.' He is still alive, but Skytrain died without getting even a toehold in the EEC's air markets.

The member governments of the EEC, other than Britain, simply do not want any of this talk of more competition, especially when it is coming from an outsider. They do not want to see their national airlines hurt, or the subsidies that governments would have to hand over to uncompetitive airlines increased. Even the British would not go that far.

That did not stop Laker. He had finally signed a firm contract for three Airbuses for $131 million in February 1981. He had beaten the British Government in court twice before. Now all he had to do was to beat nine governments at once, if necessary taking his case to the European Court of Justice at Luxembourg. The law was clearly on his side as far as everybody but the EEC's member governments were concerned. Laker's first move was to apply to the British CAA for routes into Europe to thirty-seven cities, all to be operated at low fares. He then permutated all thirty-seven cities into a network of some 630 practical routes to interconnect them. This is considered unacceptable under established monopoly practice, which bans the airline of a third country from operating a scheduled service between two other nations. Restricting an airline to operating there-and-back runs (for example, for a particular BA jet from London to Paris and then back to London, and then to Frankfurt and back) adds to costs and hence to higher fares. In the United States, federal law prevents such a block to interstate traffic and trade. That means that airlines can pick the most efficient routing from city to city, so getting many more hours a day of use out of their investment in expensive airliners. Laker was trying to do the same thing within the EEC. It sounded simple, but was politically impossible.

The CAA rejected his application. Trade Department lawyers (successors to those same lawyers who had advised Peter Shore years earlier) reckoned that there was no case to be made that the Treaty of Rome rendered the whole of the EEC's aviation regulatory machinery redundant. On a more practical level the DoT also rejected Laker's case because it was inadequately backed by economic argument on any one route, let alone for the 630-odd actually involved. The law requires that submissions should consider the economic effect of an application on other airlines. Trade Secretary John Nott went along with the CAA, though he was still interested in encouraging competition with low fares where this was possible.

The following year, there was an unprecedented piece of collaboration between Laker and Nott's successor at the Department of Trade, John Biffen, who was just as interested in getting more competition on the airlanes. With Biffen's open encouragement, Laker went to the High Court in London to get a ruling on whether the Treaty of Rome requires free competition in air transport. This prodded the EEC's Commission (its central secretariat) into taking some action. In July 1981, the ECC's competition Commissioner, Frans Andriessen, took the first steps along the road of legal action against airlines and governments for breaking anti-trust rules. That failed miserably; a supporting tour in Europe by a British junior Minister, Ian Sproat, raised the hackles of all the other Governments. One EEC Commission notion, to change the rules so that only the national government of the airline concerned should be needed to license a carrier, was vetoed in December 1981. Such a change would have prevented other countries from blocking a disruptive carrier like Laker or Denmark's Sterling Airways from entering their markets. Two other ideas—that fares should be related to costs, and that the EEC Commission should be the final arbitrator in disputes between member countries on air fares—were far too revolutionary. They would have taken power away from national governments and they were killed in meetings of civil servants from West Germany, Belgium, Italy and Denmark.

Laker did win one route for a scheduled service into Europe. Ironically, it was not to an EEC member country but to Switzerland. In March 1981, Laker Airways was given BA's route from Gatwick to Zurich. Even more ironical was the way the British authorities went in to bat for Laker over cheap air fares and persuaded the Swiss Government and Swissair to agree to lower fares. That really must have caused pain. Laker had been due to begin this operation only in 1982, just weeks after he went broke.

So, not only did Laker have more DC-10s than he needed but, during this latter part of his operations, he also had three A300s to occupy. One was swapped for two aged BAC 1-11s on his operation with Flug Union, a big tour operator working out of West Berlin. The other two were put into inclusive tour operations in Europe, where Laker slashed margins to the bone. His answer to rivals who criticized the way that he was killing all their profits during 1981 was that the Airbus was so much more efficient to operate than their older jets that he could afford to cut prices that way.

There was a steady change in the character of Laker Airways' scheduled services between the first Skytrain operation in 1977 and those running at the end. The original idea of a low-cost, no-frills service soon went by the board. By 1978, in addition to being allowed to sell tickets at least the day before, Laker began to sell through travel agents at 8 per cent commission. By 1980 a normal bookable economy ticket and an advance purchase ticket had been added, with meals included. During the summer of 1981, Laker Airways had added what it called Regency Class, a businessman's service that was essentially first-class. It was to make commercials to advertise this service that Laker took Concorde to New York during the final week of his desperate efforts to find a solution to his financial troubles. In a complete reversal of his earlier philosophy, Laker explained that now his airline would 'carry fewer passengers for more money'. The airline had also grown immensely in staff. It had begun back in 1966 with 120 people. It died in 1982 employing around 2,800.

10 · Buying big paid off before

Laker's experience since the Second World War had been that buying too many aircraft and spares had always paid off in the end. One of his first deals of any size was to buy twelve Haltons from BOAC for £42,000. These aircraft were converted wartime Halifax bombers that had been stripped of gun turrets and had cargo-carrying panniers added beneath what had been the bomb-bay. Laker had been lent £38,000 to pull off the deal by a friend, Bobby Sanderson, who owed him a favour. With this deal came what turned out to be an all-important mass of spares, especially for the aircraft's Rolls-Royce Merlin engines. He acquired these aircraft just in time for the start of the Berlin airlift, which began in June 1948 and ran for just over a year. Laker's aircraft actually were operated by Bond Air Services, using six of the Haltons at first and later six more, with half the contract fee paid by the British Government going to Laker.

The private effort on the lift was tiny in comparison with the military one, especially by the US services. The small, independent British air carriers, many of which got their start during this year, contributed just 6 per cent of the total 2.3 million tonnes lifted and Laker's aircraft one-eighth of that private-sector contribution. Laker made most of his profit from the lift not from leasing out his aircraft, but from supplying spares and aircraft servicing to the other private carriers to keep them in the air.

When the airlift finished, Bond went broke and Laker turned for a time to breaking up ex-wartime bombers for scrap. In one lucky deal (the Air Ministry was glad to get any money back at all for surplus wartime machines) Laker purchased a single job lot consisting of 99 Halifax bombers and no less than 6,000 Merlin engines. Later, in 1953, he purchased the whole of BOAC's fleet of unpopular Avro Tudor aircraft. This type had suffered several crashes, some of them unexplained. The Government eventually withdrew its licence to carry passengers, so BOAC turned them into freighters. Laker and his engineers could not see what was wrong with the Tudor that could not be fixed. Besides, the aircraft were attractive to him because they were cheap, and he could not afford to buy any better aircraft then available. The supply of cheap ex-wartime conversions was beginning to dry up. With the Tudors had come another large batch of Rolls-Royce Merlin engines (including eighty-odd new ones) and spare parts. Laker now had what amounted to a corner in the Merlin market. He had (and still has) a high reputation as a good manager of engineers. He even became a supplier of spare parts for these engines to Rolls-Royce itself. Another example of Laker's technical standing was that when he acquired three Vikings from BEA and fixed them up, it was BOAC, then a separate corporation, that bought them from Laker. His company, by then called Aviation Traders, had also successfully gone into subcontracting to the airframe makers.

One of the problems with the Tudor for use as a freighter was that it had only a very small door to allow goods in and out. Laker solved that problem by cutting a large freight-handling door in the side. He turned that idea to good use years later, when he headed BUA, with the VC-10 jets he ordered in 1961. He had shaken the rest of the British industry with his very large order for these jets— the more so since it included ten BAC 1-11s, which were still on the drawing-board when he placed the order. This large slice of business for the British aircraft industry had been used as a way of persuading Parliament to favour his efforts as head of BUA to get that airline scheduled routes, initially to West Africa. Nobody was sure how he would make profitable use of all that equipment, especially since the licences were heavily restricted. The carrying of first-class passengers was banned, for instance. To fill the space, Laker decided to carry freight. A large cargo door was added to the normal front door of all four BUA VC-10s, big enough to allow a large car or piece of machinery in and out. Laker's engineers also came up with a scissor-lift to make ground handling easier. The cargo doors, then a novelty, but now commonplace, and the freight they allowed the VC-10s to carry, turned loss-making routes into profitable ones.

Laker had an eye for what could be done with an aircraft to fit a market. Take the Carvair, a conversion of the piston-engined Douglas DC-4. Car ferries using the ugly Bristol Freighter, a bulbous twin-engined aircraft with large clamshell doors at the front, had been all the rage for the short flight across the English Channel. But by 1960 they were wearing out and were becoming uneconomical. By cutting the entire front off second-hand DC-4s, replacing it with a door that swung to one side and then relocating the cockpit high on top of the fuselage, Laker devised a low-cost replacement with longer range and better economics. Car air ferries have since dropped out of fashion, but Laker's Carvairs are still in use, for example carrying aluminium wheels from a foundry in southern California to General Motors' plant in Detroit.

He had other good ideas that did not pay off—at least not for him. He experimented with a hovercraft between Merseyside and North Wales. This, the first scheduled service using this amazing British invention, showed that hovercraft had potential, but still required years of development. The Vickers-built machine BUA used constantly broke down. Another venture based on an idea ahead of its time was his attempt to build an airliner from scratch, the Accountant. This was based on two Rolls-Royce Dart turboprop engines (of the sort used on the highly successful four-engined Vickers Viscount) to create a replacement for the ubiquitous DC-3 Dakota. The design began with an overly complicated structure of stretch-formed stressed skins, which was eventually dropped in favour of a heavier, but more conventional structure. The shape of the Accountant, however, retained the long, tapered rear fuselage inherited from the original building technique which limited the payload it could carry. The £650,000 development during 1956–7 had used up most of Air Charter's spare cash; there were up to 1,000 people involved in the project at the finish.

Laker was unable to persuade the British aircraft industry to take up the idea, or the Government to fund it, though the Hawker Siddeley group later came out with the Avro 748 design, which was remarkably similar in general lines to Laker's Accountant. Using two turboprops for aircraft of this size soon became standard worldwide.

Just about the only clearcut disaster from over-buying of equipment in Laker's early career concerned his purchase of used

Percival Prentice basic trainers from the Royal Air Force. In 1956 he bought all 252 still in service with the RAF, cleaned and repainted them and installed four-channel radios, to sell for £1,500 apiece as private aviation aircraft. They were large and heavy and were no match for the new American light aircraft then entering the market, and only a score were sold. He crawled out of this potentially costly error in 1958, when he sold Air Charter and its sister company Aviation Traders to Airwork, and that company took the trainers off his hands as part of the deal.

The negotiations with BAC over their 1-11 also taught him how to take advantage of an aircraft maker in trouble. The VC-10 had not sold very well. It had been designed for the short and often hot and high runways of Britain's colonies; the rest of the world preferred Boeing's 707. Laying longer, concrete runways proved to be cheaper and easier than the British had thought. BAC's other new jet, which in time turned into the 1-11, was being ignored by the natural lead customer, BEA, which favoured the Hawker Siddeley Trident. Laker leaned on BAC's specification until the new twin-jet would carry at least seventy passengers from London to Malta. BAC's salesmen found that American carriers might buy if the specification was improved further, including a switch from the Rolls-Royce Avon to the Spey engine. Unlike BEA, which in those days insisted on having its jets tailored precisely to its needs, Laker was flexible about the changes. He took it out on BAC later, in the negotiations over price and conditions. Just to keep BAC on its toes, he was also negotiating in parallel with Hawker Siddeley, which at that time had up to five Tridents without customers. He wanted a lease purchase that would require no down payment and to pay as he used the aircraft, out of revenue. He did not get much change out of the Hawker Siddeley people, but he did get the deal he wanted from BAC, which was sufficiently desperate to launch the project on the basis of an order for ten from an independent airline. Laker's support for the 1-11 following two crashes during flight testing helped it to recover and to sell well—for a European jet airline—including in the United States.

Later, when he was running his own airline, he adopted the same approach in dealing with Mitsui over some DC-10s. At that time the Japanese domestic carrier, All-Nippon, a wholly-owned subsidiary of Mitsui, wanted to order DC-10s, but that policy was questioned by the Japanese Government. The nation's flag carrier,

JAL, was still deciding which three-engined widebodied jet to order, the DC-10 or the Lockheed TriStar, and it had first choice. Mitsui was under pressure from two quarters. McDonnell Douglas had agreed a favourable deal to get the order from All-Nippon, and the parent did not want to lose it; and Japan was facing one of her perennial troubles over her trade surplus with America and cancelling a large aircraft order would be regarded in Tokyo as a bad thing to do.

Then two things happened. Lockheed, in one of the world's biggest business scandals, bribed its way into obtaining the All-Nippon order. At the same time, among those trying to support the Rolls-Royce TriStar programme (a case of the left hand not knowing what the right was up to), British Prime Minister Edward Heath had made a strong pitch to the Japanese Prime Minister Takeo Fukuda in favour of All-Nippon buying the Rolls-Royce-powered TriStar. Japan felt she needed to be nice to Britain: she was out-competing her car, steel, ball bearings and television industries along with those of other European countries. Japan thought that Britain, an offshore trading nation like herself, might prove to be a friend at the court of the EEC. Lockheed's bribes were probably unnecessary: All-Nippon ordered TriStars and Laker cashed in on Mitsui's resulting misfortune. He got the first two DC-10s on what amounted to hire purchase as Mitsui financed the deals at 6 per cent over ten years. Laker claimed the sales commission for his airline and used that as his down payment. Payments were made out of revenue. Laker Airways' third DC-10, and the last All-Nippon one that Mitsui had to get rid of, had been parked for a time in the Arizona desert. Laker got even more favourable terms to take that one off the Japanese trading company's hands.

When asked about these sizeable deals, for aircraft that nobody else in the business could see how Laker was going to use, his standard answer was based on: 'It's not my money.' It wasn't; he always borrowed the lot, or near enough. And when some anxious aircraft maker (or civil servant responsible for putting up large amounts of subsidized money) pointed out that Laker Airways was a one-man band and 'what would happen if anything went wrong?' Freddie Laker would then reply: 'In that case, you'll simply get your fucking aircraft back.' He has always been known for plainly calling a spade a bloody shovel!

11 · The Airbus deal

The deal that Laker made with Airbus Industrie was no exception to his ability to negotiate the best possible terms with aircraft makers. Laker cashed in on a long-running, and complex, row between three of Britain's nationalized corporations: British Aerospace (BAe), British Airways (BA), and Rolls-Royce; the American aircraft company, Boeing; and the European consortium, Airbus Industrie, in which the French and West German aircraft industries have roughly equal shares.

Inevitably, the British Government, as well as that of both France and West Germany, was also involved. Britain in the form of Hawker Siddeley, had dropped out of the consortium as a partner some years earlier, because the British Government would not fund its stake. The company had, however, as a part of BAe, continued to build the wings of the Airbus A300 at its Chester factory. A lengthy debate began in 1977 about whether BAe should rejoin Airbus Industrie or, instead, do a deal with Boeing. The American giant, which has built more jet airliners than all the rest of the West's aircraft makers put together (including McDonnell Douglas and Lockheed) was proposing that BAe should become the lead risk-sharing subcontractor in the project that became Boeing's 757 model. BAe's management, led by ex-MP and former Labour Party Industry Minister Lord Beswick, did not want this because it feared being squashed by Boeing's strictly commercial attitudes. Complicating the whole matter in the 1977-8 period was that Rolls-Royce was trying to get its RB211 big-fan engine (the 535 version) adopted by Boeing for the 757. Meanwhile, BA, needing a new, more fuel-efficient aircraft, was leaning in favour of the Boeing 757 rather than the Airbus, which would have overlapped BA's larger Lockheed TriStar fleet.

The French Government, the aviation industry and the French-dominated management of Airbus Industrie, who all expect nationalized industries to behave in what they see as a responsible fashion, could not understand why the British could not arrange things better. Before they would be happy to see BAe back in Airbus Industrie, as good Europeans, they wanted British Airways to order Airbuses. In later years, talking about a more recently proposed and smaller Airbus Industrie project, an executive of Air France said from the heart: 'It would have to fly backwards for us not to order.'

From Boeing's point of view, its offer to BAe eventually became generous. It would allow 60 per cent of the work on the 757 to be done by the British in return for a like share ($300–400 million) of the airframe's fairly modest proposed development cost. At that time, it had been intended to use rather more of the existing Boeing 727 and 737 designs than actually became the case, to keep development costs down to levels that BAe and the British Government could afford. The Americans, who habitually take on staff and lay them off as the production rate of aircraft is varied to suit market demand, were even prepared to organize a more constant approach to production—at a price. The British Government would have had to come up with a subsidy to cover the extra costs this constant rate would incur. The president of Boeing's commercial aircraft division was Tex Boullion, a quietly spoken man from Arkansas. He was concerned that without a transatlantic deal of some sort, Europe's one-third or so of the world's airliner market could become locked away behind a protectionist wall in order to help Airbus Industrie.

Boeing also had reasons closer to home that had led it to look for a risk-sharing partner in the 757. It was already planning to launch the larger 210-seat 767 model at an initial cost of $1.3 billion or so. That project was absorbing most of Boeing's spare engineers. Back in the early 1970s, Boeing had been forced to sack a large number of its engineering staff when orders slumped for its new 747 jumbo. It did not want to be forced into a similar position again—having to take on staff in order to cope with two development programmes in parallel, only to sack them later, when the work ran out. It had taken a lot of criticism in the early 1970s and the memory was still fresh. The British aviation industry was the only one outside the

United States that had the ready-made ability to take on the Boeing work.

The commercial advantages of the proposed Boeing deal for BAe were appealing. They meant involvement in a civil airliner project that might make a commercial return on the initial investment, plus providing the opportunity for the British aircraft industry's employees to learn from perhaps the world's best organized maker of civil jets. No British jet airliner, including the BAC 1-11, which sold 230, has ever repaid its initial investment in full.

Boeing's proposal was pushed hard, among others by the *Economist*, and it had a handful of allies in Whitehall, too, but BAe's management was intransigent. The management and the unions trumpeted that all Boeing was really interested in was killing off BAe's ability to design airliners and to turn it into a captive and submissive subcontractor. In fact, the biggest airliner that BAe can ever hope to launch alone is the BAe 146 feederliner, with 80–100 seats—and then only because the Government put up almost all of the initial investment.

In due course, the arguments and squabbling between the state-owned corporations reached a sufficient pitch for it to occupy a fair amount of government time. The Prime Minister, Callaghan, eventually decided to take over the Cabinet subcommittee looking into the matter. In late June 1978, when he was in Washington to receive the first Hubert Humphrey award, he took the opportunity to investigate what the Americans were up to. He had separate talks with T. A. 'Tug' Wilson, Boeing's chairman, Frank Borman, the astronaut boss of Eastern Airlines (a leading customer for Boeing's 757 and Sandy McDonnell, of McDonnell Douglas. Craftily, McDonnell Douglas dressed up what amounted to a spoiling bid into a proposal that looked more like a permanent, long-term arrangement, possibly leading to other civil projects. Boeing's was strictly a for-profit, one-off contract on the 757; anything else would have to be negotiated separately. McDonnell Douglas, one of the world's leading fighter makers, already had a link with BAe over the development of the vertical takeoff Harrier. A study of the McDonnell Douglas outline proposal was arranged by the British, but achieved only a further delay. (Ironically, the day after Laker Airways went into receivership in 1982, McDonnell Douglas ended another lengthy study, this time with the Dutch aircraft company, Fokker. They had been looking into building jointly a 150-seat airliner.)

During the summer of 1978, Rolls-Royce's case became much more urgent. Its was the preferred lead engine on the 757 for both Eastern and British Airways, assuming the British carrier was allowed to order. If the airliner was to be launched on time, to enter service late in 1982, there was little time left to begin the engine development, which takes longer than for the airframe. Rolls also needed at least a $500 million commitment from the British Government to cover the development cost of the RB211-535. A problem for the Government was that there was no obvious alternative role for the RB211 engine in Europe. Yet there were more jobs involved in building the RB211 than in building Airbus wings at BAe. An additional factor in all this was that BA needed to replace its ageing fleet of Tridents and, as an interim step, wanted to buy Boeing 737s; that contract would be less costly if it was also tied to an eventual order for Boeing 757s.

Britain's Foreign Secretary, Dr David Owen, wanted BAe to join Airbus Industrie because that would have been a good, pro-European thing to do. Most of his foreign policy to that point had been dominated by the American connection. Owen was supported by the Employment Secretary, Albert Booth, an uncomplicated, ruddy-faced man whose views on this, as on everything else, were influenced by the trade unions. Industry Secretary Eric Varley sat on the fence as usual; his normal indecision was made worse because two of his charges, BAe and RR, were pulling in opposite directions. Trade Secretary Edmund Dell listened to BA, which was in his charge, and supported Boeing, the more so since its offer made better commercial sense. In the end, a large part in the eventual outcome was played by West Germany's Chancellor, Helmut Schmidt, at two summit meetings in July 1978. He stood on Britain's side, against the French, making it clear that he understood that there were more jobs (and more trade, in dollars) on offer to Britain from Rolls-Royce's deal with Boeing than from any BAe deal with Airbus Industrie. The Euroconsortium had only managed to get one order in America, from Eastern Airlines, and then only with what amounted to give-away finance. To add weight to this argument, one month later, in August, United Airlines chose Boeing's other new project, the 767, over the Airbus. The French remained adamant. They wanted

BAe back in Airbus Industrie as what is still called a 'full' partner, though with only a 20 per cent stake, and to pay a share of past and future investment. But there was a strict condition: British Airways must first order the Airbus. Any problem this might cause Rolls-Royce was no concern of France. Any counter-argument that when it had suited her France too had done deals with the Americans, in computers, even jet engines with General Electric, cut no ice whatever.

The Farnborough Air Show in early September 1978 proved to be an even more frenetic hotbed of rumour than usual. Only this time, at least one of the stories being peddled was true. Laker Airways was going to order ten Airbuses, and the story was being leaked heavily by none other than Rolls-Royce's chairman, Sir Kenneth Keith. And so it proved. Towards the end of September, Laker did order ten Airbus A300-B4s, along with five more long-range DC-10s to add to the six the airline already had.

This order, which had not been considered as a possibility in any of the earlier Government discussions of BAe's plan to buy back into Airbus Industrie, or even in Cabinet committee, became crucial in the last stage of manoeuvring to square this circle. The Prime Minister, Callaghan, had decided that the only solution was to allow the three state-owned corporations to make their own decision. British Airways followed its inclination and added to its order for 19 Boeing 737s a purchase of 19 plus 18 options for the Boeing 757. (Eastern Airlines announced on the same day that it was ordering 27 plus 24 options of the 757.) Rolls-Royce's RB211-535 engine was chosen by both lead customers. At the same time, BAe announced its intention of buying back into the Airbus consortium, provided the French would agree. It was to pay as its entry price the £50 million maximum allowed for such adventures under the Act that had nationalized the British aircraft industry. On top of that, BAe was to pay 20 per cent of the expected $850 million launch cost of the new version of the Airbus, the A310. This cost has since risen to at least $1 billion. BAe also had to renegotiate the lucrative, guaranteed contract it had to build A300 wings, which was replaced by an unguaranteed one involving all the risks that go with being a full partner.

The crucial question was: would the French accept Laker Airway's order as a sufficient face saver—as an order from a British airline, even though not from BA itself? BA's chairman was leaned on by Ministers. Its chairman, Lord McFadzean, said: 'Any future requirement for widebodied aircraft of medium size and range could most satisfactorily be met by the A310.' Everybody in the business knew that BA had no intention whatever of buying Airbuses, but it relieved tensions. 'It was an emotional thing at the time,' BAe's Jim Thorne explains. 'British Airways' refusal to order Airbuses was, from a French point of view, utterly illogical. We needed some British airline business to lend credibility to our approach to Airbus.' From BAe's point of view, Laker's order was manna from heaven. Under pressure from the West German Government, which wanted to share its role as the main paymaster for the enormously expensive Airbus project, the French reluctantly conceded.

An outside point of view was that the French had little choice, however awkward they were in the meantime. The British had designed the wings for both the A300 and the new A310 version and had the only factory outside the United States capable of putting them together efficiently, using automated equipment. There was no other aircraft maker in the world with spare capacity to take on the work. A boom in airliner ordering was just beginning, following the boom in air travel that had started in 1977. A question arose whether, if BAe had done a deal with Boeing, it could also have retained the wing-building contract for both Airbuses. The French reckoned that the wings of the new A310 version could just as well be built in Germany, and the Germans were keen to try. The British, however, had the trump card, in the shape of already installed automated equipment. A tougher approach at the top of BAe might conceivably have pulled off such a coup, but its ex-politician chairman, Lord Beswick, proved to be a weak leader, unable to stand up to pressure from the unions and his own managers.

There was a genuine, and typical, overlay of patriotism in Laker's announcement of the Airbus order. Thundering against British Government policy, Laker said: 'It's a terrible indictment that I'm having to buy a new aircraft built abroad rather than in Britain', thus neatly insulting BAe to whose aid he had just come. Laker was also embarrassed to be reminded by journalists at the time of the order that he had earlier damned the Airbus as likely to be useless, since it would be like a horse designed by a committee and would therefore fly like a camel. The role of Rolls-Royce's Sir

Kenneth Keith in all this became clear when Laker said that he still hoped to put Rolls-Royce engines on his Airbuses. It sounded good even if it made no sense. Laker Airways' DC-10s used basically the same General Electric engines as the Airbus, so saving on spares and maintenance costs. And, since these engines were being traded across national borders, government-subsidized export finance would be available for GE's engines; Rolls-Royce was in no position to finance anything. Rolls was even insisting that in the unlikely event that the RB211 were to be adapted to fit the Airbus, the British Government would have to put up the £35 million or so that this would cost. Besides which, Rolls-Royce had a good deal arranged with Boeing and so was not much bothered about Airbus. And, it turned out, neither was the British Government. Airbuses now fly with engines made by both GE and Pratt and Whitney, but not by Rolls-Royce.

Laker took typical advantage of BAe's weak position—and the Government's willingness to support the nationalized airframe maker—to carve out a good deal on his A300s. At least that was how it looked at the end of the negotiations in 1979. The deal was mostly worked out between Laker and Bernard Lathiere, the French ex-civil servant who heads Airbus Industrie. At $42 million apiece for the first three, Laker did not get a special base price for the Airbuses, but he did claim and get some financial help as the launch customer in Britain. Laker Airways received letters of credit for goods and services such as training. A normal sales contract with Airbus Industrie includes training for, say, one and a half flight crews per aircraft. Laker got three crews trained for the same purchase price. He also received letters of credit covering spare parts and ground equipment from outside vendors, which were in effect paid for by Airbus Industrie. The normal up-front payment of 10 per cent was put back from the date of the firm order until the day of delivery, when Laker paid it with interest added at normal commercial rates; the other 90 per cent came from a syndicate of thirteen banks organized by the Midland Bank. In all, Laker got something like £7 million off what he should have paid for the first three Airbuses, and this just happened, roughly speaking, to equal the initial down payment that should have been made on the first three. Once again, Laker had made a cashless aircraft purchase, with the supplier indirectly funding the down payment that normally goes with the order.

Financing the deal with Laker Airways was not easy. Even before the Airbus contract was negotiated in detail in January 1981, for $131 million in all, including spare parts, the airline's balance sheet was in pretty stretched shape. The accounts for the year to March 1980 showed that Laker had made £801,000 profit before tax, on revenue of £82·5 million. But the accounts also showed that there was a £13·9 million excess of current liabilities over net current assets and £111·4 million of long-term loans outstanding against a total capitalization of £5 million or so (including just £510,000 of fully paid-up share capital). The company was already highly geared by any standards. The pressure to lend money to Laker was, however, sufficient to overcome any normal banking industry reluctance.

Midland's name had come out of the hat when it was time for BAe to select its lead British bank to finance its 20 per cent share of all Airbus sales. (Barclays had at that time won second prize with the BAe 146.) Midland assumed this role in March 1979. By the end of the first year, it had taken on about $900 million in commitments, including the Laker deal. Midland had little choice. If it wanted this business, which it obviously did, then, BAe told the bank in a sharply worded letter, it had to take the rough with the smooth. It is a common problem for banks involved in financing an aircraft company's sales that they are reluctant to take on the risky deals along with the good ones.

Midland had some idea what it was up against in the case of the Laker deal, though. Robert L. Wyatt, corporate finance director of the Midland, told a conference in Holland in August 1980:

> The commercial airlines in Europe are a different and more difficult case [to lend to]. We have a number of them in the UK. Sir Freddie Laker has done an extraordinary job of flying people across the Atlantic. He now has ten or eleven DC-10s, all of which he has purchased in the last three or four years. Now he has purchased three A300s. The amount of money involved there is vast. His capital resources are not vast.

There had also been some discreet pressure from the British Government to see that the finance was made available to Laker for the Airbus sale. And the British Government smoothed the way forward through an overt commitment in the form of an interest-rate subsidy. The $131 million loan was made in dollars, a fatal mistake as it eventually transpired, and the Government agreed to keep the actual net interest rate Laker would pay to 10·2 per cent. The Midland arranged an international syndicate of banks, all of whom were encouraged by the boom in the aviation business and the British Government's helping hand. Surprisingly, it seems, with the advantage of hindsight, the Airbus loan was oversubscribed.

And so the final piece was laid in the jigsaw that led in 1982 to Laker's bankruptcy.

12 · Out of his depth

In the past, something had always turned up to rescue Laker from the effects of whatever excess capacity he had saddled his airline with. But the deepening world recession in 1980–1 blocked any chance of some unexpected market emerging to save him, just at the time when he had contracted to take on so many DC-10s and Airbuses. The North Atlantic market for scheduled passengers went flat. The market decline was nowhere near as severe as in 1975, following the OPEC oil-price increase, when the total number of passengers crossing the North Atlantic actually went down. But there was no growth of any sort.

In 1974 and 1975, there was a decline in the total number of passengers flying across the North Atlantic. In 1975, the total fell to below 12½ million, 5 per cent less than the year before. Soon the Western world's economy began to recover from the oil shock and as it did, so did air travel. There was an 11 per cent increase in the number of passengers travelling across the Atlantic in 1976, an improvement that faltered in the first part of the next year, but turned into the start of an unprecedented boom towards the end of the year that continued into 1978. Compared with the year before, the number of North Atlantic passengers in 1978 increased by no less than 28 per cent. This was the first year of Laker's Skytrain and the boom no doubt helped it to make immediate profits.

Just as the American authorities had feared, the new and highly competitive fares that the scheduled carriers introduced in parallel with Skytrain severely hurt the charter operators. In this period their market share had peaked in 1977, with 28 per cent of all passengers on the North Atlantic. That share began an immediate and permanent decline. In 1981, the charter operators had less than a 10 per cent market share.

The boom in air travel across the Atlantic continued into 1979, with a 15 per cent increase overall. However, Laker's ability to participate in this was hit by the six-week grounding of the DC-10 world fleet, following the disastrous crash of an American Airlines DC-10 at Chicago. Since then, the West's economy has slipped back into recession. OPEC increased oil prices again in 1979 and as economic growth faltered, so did air travel, though not as badly as back in 1974–5. In 1981 there was still 1·5 per cent overall growth in the number of passengers carried (made up from a 3·5 per cent increase in the number of passengers carried on scheduled services, including Skytrain, and a 14 per cent decline in the number of charter passengers).

The world's airlines were losing money as they had not done since the early 1970s, when they had over-purchased widebodied jets like the Boeing 747, the Lockheed TriStar and the DC-10. The airlines had believed that the earlier years of steady growth averaging 12–15 per cent a year would continue. IATA reckons that its members flying the North Atlantic lost $600 million on that route alone in 1981—and close to $1 billion world-wide. They therefore began to compete harder than ever for passengers, cutting fares to loss-making levels to win market share at any price. Getting some cash through their tills became of paramount importance.

This was the climate in which Laker found himself awash in capacity that he did not need and could not afford. For the first time in his history in the business, there were no markets that he could turn to—he was out of his depth.

13 · Anatomy of the collapse

May 1979 brought two blows for Laker. His mother, to whom he had always been very close, died; and, following the crash of an American Airlines DC-10 in Chicago, the American authorities grounded everybody's DC-10s. That included Laker's, right at the start of the peak holiday traffic season.

The Chicago crash was the worst single aviation accident in United States history, killing all 274 people aboard. It was an emotional event, and at first nobody was clear about what had gone wrong. One early theory, founded on false evidence, was that some bolts had failed and the engine mounted on the left wing had fallen off. There was no doubt that the left-wing engine had torn away and flown back over the top of the wing. The slats—surfaces that extend from the front of the wing to increase lift during take-off and landing, matching flaps that do the same thing at the rear of the wing—on the left side had retracted. The tearing caused by the departing engine had ripped through the hydraulic circuits that held the slats open. With less lift from the wing, the aircraft rolled over and into the ground. The pilot did not know what had happened and so was unable to prevent the catastrophe.

Subsequent investigation showed that the cause was appalling maintenance errors by American Airlines. The company had found it was quicker to remove the wing engines on the DC-10 in one piece, complete with the pylon that mounted them onto the wing—and was doing so with a fork-lift truck. The correct way to do the job was to separate the engine from the pylon and use a special lowering jig, which took longer and was more costly. The misalignments caused by using something as crude as a fork lift truck, both on removal and then on reassembly, had cracked the brackets that attached the pylon to the wing.

The administrator of the Federal Aviation Administration, Langhorne Bond, wasted no time—in fact, he shot over-rapidly from the hip. He grounded all DC-10s almost immediately. After some investigation suggested that the problem might not be as general as was first feared, he allowed them to fly again, but with frequent inspections. When these began to show up cracks on other airlines' DC-10s, he once again grounded all 138 of the type registered in the United States for what turned out to be six weeks. In safety matters, the world's leading aviation countries stick together. The British CAA matched what the Americans did, even when it became clear that such a blanket action was not strictly necessary. The American's caution was understandable, however, since this was not the first time the DC-10 had been in trouble. Earlier, the cause of a crash in Paris in 1974 had been in the design of a luggage-bay door lock; the problem had been identified before the crash, but had been shushed up through a gentleman's agreement between the FAA and the DC-10's maker, McDonnell Douglas. Mr Bond wanted no such scandal to mar his term as FAA administrator. To make matters worse for Laker, it eventually emerged that when his DC-10s needed maintenance in the United States, this work had been contracted to American Airlines. Careful inspection showed no signs of any similar damage to Laker Airways aircraft.

Reducing its long-haul fleet to two tired Boeing 707s left Laker Airways with no choice. Skytrain was cancelled until further notice, reducing the company's revenue to that coming in from inclusive tours. This did not completely eliminate profits for the year to March 1980, as Laker feared it might immediately after the grounding. But it did cut profits from the £2 million pre-tax on revenues of £90 million in the year to March 1979 to £801,000 pre-tax on revenues of £82·5 million in the year to March 1980. Laker reckoned that the six-week grounding during what was still a healthy travel market had cost the carrier £13 million in revenues. Skytrain's revenues for the year were reduced to below those from the company's inclusive tour business. While Laker still had at this time no short-term borrowings or overdraft, cash in hand (made up of deposits for holidays, etc.) at the end of the 1979–80 financial year was down from the expected £11 million to £6 million. Laker pooh-poohed the idea that the grounding might cause his airline severe financial strain: 'The strength of our balance sheet will see us through,' he said. 'No, I am not bust!' With travel still booming, he was right. The balance sheet was strong enough to get through this crisis, despite having recently taken on $59 million in debt to Mitsui (at 8·5 per cent) for two more DC-10s during the early part of 1979. Later that year Laker had also contracted to borrow $228 million, at rates varying from 6 per cent to 9 per cent over nine years with banks led by America's Export-Import Bank, to buy another five DC-10s. And it did not stop him from concluding the negotiations early in 1981 to raise $131 million to buy his first three Airbuses.

The first clear public sign that the reputed strength of Laker's balance sheet was not all that it might seem came in August 1981 through an article in the *Sunday Telegraph*. This revealed that Laker was attempting to renegotiate the repayment schedule on the Exim loan. The airline had managed to meet the payments for the first six months of its financial year, but could not see how it would find the $48 million repayment of interest and principal needed between September 1981 and March 1982, on total borrowings of $400 million or so. Laker's problem was that virtually all of his debt was in dollars while approaching two-thirds of his revenue was in pounds. When the loans had been arranged the pound had been strong; now it was weak. In mid-August, it sank as low as $1·78, which represented a decline of more than one-quarter since he had taken out the loans. What that meant to Laker was that his airline had to earn at least one-quarter more pounds to be able to repay the debts than he had budgeted for.

Offensively, Laker told the bankers that he was going to teach them their jobs, which did not help his case one bit. 'I have innovated in aviation; now I must innovate in banking,' he boasted. What he had in mind was what he called a 'release and recapture' clause that he wanted added to the contracts. This would have allowed him to put off the repayments for a time and for the bankers to reclaim (or recapture) those delayed repayments later. It wasn't exactly welshing on the loans, more a variation on rescheduling. As a stop-gap, he put up the airline's two old Boeing 707s and the four BAC 1-11s for sale on the second-hand market. For scrap the 707s together might have raised $1 million and the 1-11s less than $1 million each, even though they were in good condition.

The storm clouds gathered. Traffic on the North Atlantic had been sagging since the beginning of 1981 as the world's economy slid further into recession. Concerned that the position of Laker Airways was getting even worse than it had suspected, the CAA began to monitor its fortunes. In March, Laker had tried to lead the way to raising fares on the North Atlantic routes to New York, Los Angeles and to Miami. The big carriers waited to see what Laker would do with his cheap fares that had formed the floor on which all other fares were erected. He pushed them up by 11–33 per cent. Laker also devised some hidden fare increases by changing the timing of the seasonal changeover from winter to peak fares, and by shortening the intermediate fare period when what are called 'shoulder' fares would be available. Traffic was already depressed and most of the major airlines were declaring monster losses that were growing larger quarter by quarter. Nevertheless, the major airlines followed Laker's suit. There was an immediate reaction from potential passengers; bookings dropped sharply. So Laker quickly pushed fares back down again whence they had come and the majors just as promptly followed suit. Large fare increases of the sort that had been tried were 'a mistake', said Laker. As the *Economist* pointed out in March, Laker Airways 'put up its fares mightily because of the interest burden on its debt for a handsome fleet of new aircraft'. Lowering the fares again left the airline with its original problem, that of paying the interest, unsolved.

By August, when Laker began pleading for time to make his payments on his massive loans, the CAA was issuing private warnings to other government Departments. The load factors on Laker's Skytrain services still looked reasonable; they actually averaged almost 78 per cent in the five months to October 1981 (i.e., through this period), but there was a steady decline from the year before. Worse, the normal summer holiday peak failed to materialize to the expected extent. These loads were not sufficient to raise the sorts of sums of money that Laker needed. And while his tour business was profitable it was not generating enough for Laker Airways to cope. Soundings were taken by CAA officials with the Treasury, the Industry and Trade Departments, and with the Bank of England.

Laker's troubles centred on the two big loans for the DC-10s and the Airbuses. The former was arranged by McDonnell Douglas, which made the aircraft, and General Electric, which made the engines. It was a fairly conventional deal, backed by United States Government export finance. At the time of the bankruptcy, about $24 million had been paid off from the $228 million loan, which was arranged in three parts, all to run over nine years. The government Exim Bank loaned $86·8 million at 8⅜ per cent directly from its own funds. It also guaranteed $74·5 million raised by the Private Export Funding Corporation (which raises finance in the private sector for government-approved export deals). The rest, $67 million, was raised by a group of banks and financial organizations: Morgan Guaranty, $21 million; Marine Midland, $10 million; Royal Bank of Canada, with Clydesdale Bank, $11 million; National Westminster, $4 million; McDonnell Douglas' export finance subsidiary, $14 million; and General Electric's Credit Corporation, $7 million. In addition, the two manufacturers undertook what is known as a first-loss guarantee, which would mean their making up for the first 25 per cent of the cost to the lenders if the aircraft were ever sold at a loss.

The Exim Bank had been under pressure from the Reagan administration over the amount of money that export finance consumed to subsidize aircraft sales abroad. The last thing it wanted was to be faced with a foreclosure on a large loan, so it proved to be accommodating to Laker. The airline paid the interest but Exim agreed to defer the capital payment for thirty days, otherwise due in September, solely on the understanding that Laker Airways' other major loans syndicate would accept its share of the problem.

The loan that had been created to finance the Airbus deal had some interesting twists to it that only emerged as Laker's troubles grew. Led by Midland Bank, a syndicate involving twelve other banks had raised the money. Airbus Industrie had agreed to the standard 25 per cent first-loss guarantee. The $131 million loan over ten years was at market rates, as far as the lenders were concerned. But so anxious was the British Government to see that the Laker order for Airbuses did not go astray that it not only leant on Midland to come up with the money, but also agreed to subsidize it. The market interest rate was to be subsidized down to a constant 10·2 per cent. Mrs Thatcher's Government always maintained that there was no government money involved in this Airbus deal; that was true as far as cash was concerned, but it was untrue in fact. Just as Laker could not meet the payment due to

Exim in September, he could not meet the one that was to go to the Midland syndicate. Technically, Laker was in default on the Midland-syndicate loan and the contract said that in this event the interest-rate subsidy would terminate. The Government stepped in and, after lengthy consultations with the Bank of England, the payment was postponed and the subsidy continued untouched.

The Bank was disturbed with what it was finding out about the way that Laker's finances had been managed and about the airline's lack of financial management. Officials at the Bank prompted Midland Bank to provide Laker Airways with some financial advisors. The problem was who? It was already pretty obvious to those with access to the figures that Laker Airways was broke and probably beyond rescue; that meant there would perhaps be no fee at the end of the day. So Midland turned to its own wholly-owned merchant bank, Samuel Montagu. One of its managing directors, Ian McIntosh, was given the thankless task of seeing what could be done. As he explains: 'When the Bank [of England] asks, bankers do.' He admits there was some argument during the early autumn about Montagu's independence from others involved in the Laker mess. Most of that talk soon disappeared. However, many in the City believe that Samuel Montagu's firm stand, often against what the Midland might have hoped for, has done it little good with its parent.

Prudence dictated an increase in the bond that was posted to cover Laker's holiday companies should anything go wrong. The Clydesdale Bank, which was actually Laker's long-standing bank and also a wholly-owned subsidiary of Midland, in October increased Laker Airways' holiday company bond with the CAA to £5 million. Clydesdale also started to allow Laker to draw on an overdraft facility.

October proved to be a month of comings and goings with not too much to show for all the efforts being expended on Laker's behalf by the banks and aircraft makers and especially by Ian McIntosh. Because of quiet but intense lobbying by the British Government in Washington, the Exim Bank agreed to a second, but final, thirty-day extension to the principal payment. In return, however, the Americans set a deadline of 17 November for the other syndicate to come up with some concrete proposals as to what it would agree to do to let Laker Airways off the hook.

Laker's initial tack during this period was a typical one—all he had to do was sell one of the three Airbuses in his fleet. The efficient aircraft, then the newest of the widebodied jets, were still in demand, he reckoned, and would raise enough to get him out of the woods until traffic picked up again. It was possible that he could profitably have sold the order positions for the Airbuses in the immediate period after he had signed the firm contract in early 1981. The travel recession was only just beginning to bite at that time. But by November the aircraft would have been worth no more than half book value for an instant sale. Eastern Airlines had picked up two almost new Airbuses for $42 million each in early 1980. Laker's financial advisors also found a much more important snag in the small print of the contract, something it seemed, that Laker was not even aware existed. If one of the Airbuses was sold, the interest-rate subsidy would end on all three. Laker could not afford to pay market rate and so that idea died. Merchant bank Samuel Montagu also was convinced that any idea of selling immediately all three Airbuses would raise other problems, since Laker had long-term contracts requiring them all for the summer of 1982. That meant either losing the business or having to charter somebody else's jets at considerable expense.

A crucial meeting took place on 4 November at Midland Bank's headquarters in the City. Men from all the banks involved in both syndicates, representatives of McDonnell Douglas, General Electric, Airbus Industrie and British Aerospace, plus the Bank of England, were gathered on one side of the boardroom. On the other was Laker with Montagu's Ian McIntosh and Bill Morrison, from the accountant firm Thomson McLintock, who had been nominated to act as finance director of the airline. There were also observers from the British Government and from America's Exim Bank. There was no choice but to agree to reschedule Laker's debts, or to force the airline into bankruptcy there and then. The question was for how long to reschedule and on what terms. The Americans were pressing the idea that it should be for only six months, or until the normal 15 March 1982 date for the half-yearly payment. That was not accepted by the others, since that would simply have pushed the problem off until Laker hit the worst period of peak borrowing for the airline. Travel is always at its lowest in February and yet that is the time that holiday companies sign firm forward contracts for hotels and the like. A subsequent compilation of all the cash-flow forecasts that were made at this time (by Orion Royal Bank, as part of its stillborn rescue attempt after the bankruptcy) showed that in March 1982, Laker Airways' cash balance was expected to be £19 million in the red, down from a positive position of £15·9 million in August 1981. This decline would come about even though Laker's holiday business by then was expected to be taking in an increasing volume of deposits on holidays, rising from almost £12 million in February 1982 to £13·5 million in March. The peak inflow of holiday prepayments was predicted for June and July that year, at £17·4 million for each month. It would have to be a twelve-month stretch-out of the repayments, or nothing.

Any slight ray of hope that some miracle might appear to save Laker was soon extinguished at that meeting. During October there had been a discreet search for a 'partner' for Laker, which was a tactful way of describing an outright takeover, leaving no more than a figurehead role for Sir Freddie Laker himself. Nobody was interested, which makes it all the stranger that *Fortune* later reported that at some point during the summer of 1981, Laker's name was considered as a suitable replacement for Bill Seawell at the head of Pan American, which was itself in deep financial trouble.

McDonnell Douglas presented to the meeting some traffic forecasts that made it look as though there might be some hope, if Laker could hang on until the following summer. The CAA dashed that idea, believing that the forecasts were much too optimistic, which was proved right by events. It came down in the end to a matter of what each creditor was prepared to do, at which point it emerged that the biggest difficulty lay with the Airbus loan.

Airbus Industrie was adamant. It would do no more than meet the contract conditions requiring it to pay for the first 25 per cent of any loss on a forced-sale of the aircraft. This was less callous than it might have seemed. The European consortium had no vast reserves of cash, but was dependent for its finances on the goodwill of governments. It was also hoping for the third time to raise a large amount of cash to launch its dreamed-about 150-seat airliner, while its existing two types, the A300 and A310 were still a long way from making any real return on the $2 billion total investment in them— and likely never will. The West German Government in particular had made clear its increasing dissatisfaction with its investment in the Airbus programme (but without being willing to pull out or refuse to invest in new programmes—such is the logic of politicians). There was also residual antipathy towards Laker because of the reluctance of the British Government to force all three of its nationalized industries to be good Europeans and back the Airbus project wholeheartedly. The Germans wanted to know why their Government should bail out Laker, at some cost to themselves, when the British had chosen to spend most of their aviation dollars with Boeing on competing programmes.

Ten of the thirteen banks in the Midland syndicate were prepared to go along with some rescheduling of this loan for up to the necessary twelve months. But three would not: the two West German banks, Dresdner Bank and Bayerische Vereinsbank, and Creditanstalt Bankverein of Austria. Their strongly expressed view was that Laker Airways was irretrievably bankrupt and that all secured creditors would get more of their money back if the airline's aircraft were sold sooner rather than later. The second-hand market for widebodied jets was already overflowing with available machines. There were at that time around 55 Boeing 747 jumbos available (not all were idle; some were still in use by their owners), at least 40 DC-10s (with many of the long-haul version parked at America's desert airfields), and the first second-hand Airbuses were beginning to be traded. The German-speaking trio, however, were clear. Waiting would mean less money back, not more; the Airbuses should therefore be put on the market immediately.

The three German and Austrian banks were under different pressures than the Americans. Exim did not want a default, for domestic reasons. McDonnell Douglas was anxious not to get its aircraft back, because there was no market for DC-10s; sales had collapsed after the Chicago crash and never recovered. However, the German banks' profits were being squeezed because of the problem with the Polish debt. Dresdner Bank, the leading West German bank in that country's share of Airbus financing, was also the lead bank for a West German Government-guaranteed $500 million debt rescue for Poland. Dresdner's profits in 1981 had already been hit.

There is another, less obvious, reason for the reluctance shown by these three banks and also Airbus Industrie. The West German national airline, Lufthansa, had at first been a reluctant customer for the Euroconsortium's aircraft, but had turned into an enthusiastic supporter. Later, Lufthansa had, with Swissair, played a crucial role in defining the specification, and then ordering, the smaller A310 version of the Airbus. Laker's attitudes and his keenness to compete openly was anathema to the orderly minds of the German airline's bosses, who have always been among the staunchest supporters of IATA. Inevitably there was pressure from the airline on the German bankers. Laker was bad enough when he was competing on the North Atlantic. His Skytrains had succeeded in ruining the neat and tidy lives of airlines such as British Airways, Pan Am and TWA, though in the Germans' minds the effect had spilled over onto their operations through the American Government's wholesale attack on IATA. Now, to make things much worse, Laker was proposing to enter the European market, or at least to make things difficult in the European Court. And he was planning to use Airbuses on these European services.

There was a ready means for passing on the German airline's views on Laker to the banking industry in that country. The long-standing honorary chairman of Lufthansa's supervisory board of directors is Dr Hermann Abs, who holds the same position with the Deutsche Bank. Even though he was approaching 80 years of age at the time of the Laker collapse, he remains a powerful man in the German system.

By comparison, the attitude of the manufacturers and banks involved in the DC-10 loan was much more conciliatory. The last thing they wanted was to push Laker over the edge. In early November the Exim Bank announced that it would agree to a twelve-month rescheduling of Laker's payments, but there was a condition. There had to be a detailed agreement by 6 January to reschedule the other, Midland-led, loan. If that was the good news for the month, the bad news came from an entirely unexpected quarter: Pan Am.

That US airline's losses had been mounting steadily during the year, and in the summer of 1981 Chase Manhattan had refused to join a $475 million revolving credit planned to run to 1 December. Instead, Chase led a challenge to the airline's chairman, Bill Seawell, and Pan Am was forced to sell off its only remaining valuable asset, the profitable Intercontinental Hotel chain, to the Grand Metropolitan group in Britain, for a net gain of $348 million. Seawell was ousted, into 'early retirement'. Pan Am's new boss was Ed Acker, fresh from another upstart airline, Air Florida, that had been growing rapidly in America's deregulated atmosphere on the back of cheap fares. On 1 November 1981, he twisted the knife hard in Laker's back by starting to sell at the lowest fares on the North Atlantic.

This was the end of Laker's special claim to fame. Acker had received an analysis of the result on the North Atlantic of Pan Am's whole range of fares, ranging from a $550 standard economy fare down to a Standby fare, more or less identical to Laker's. In fact, in the summer of 1981, Pan Am's average fare had been only $262, a lot less than Laker's unrestricted economy fare (that allowed advance booking) of $299. By October, as passengers began trading down to cheaper fares to alleviate the effects of the recession on their bank balances, Pan Am's average fare was down to $249. So Acker cut the whole thing back to three fares: first class; Clipper (or business) class; and a single, straightforward low economy fare of $261.

Just how devastating this was to prove for Laker's traffic was not immediately apparent to the bankers trying to save Laker Airways. Otherwise they might have saved themselves a lot of heartache and given in there and then. The CAA's officials feared what was going on and redoubled their monitoring of Laker's position. It was about this time that the Prime Minister, Margaret Thatcher, asked to be kept informed of progress in the rescue effort. Laker was an old family friend and was known in Whitehall as 'her Knight in a shining fuselage'. She had even gone to the trouble of giving Laker an endorsement at the Tory Party conference on 16 October. 'It is thanks to Freddie Laker that you can cross the Atlantic for so much less than it would have cost in the early 1970s,' she said. Then she added a Tory commercial: 'Competition works.' (As it does, both ways.)

There were more serious concerns about when a bankruptcy should be allowed to take place, if it should prove inevitable. Nobody wanted a repeat of the 1974 Court Line case, when direct government intervention had merely put off the evil day and had still left many voters with ruined holidays. There was no intention of giving direct aid in Laker's case—how could the Tories' entrepreneurial hero be saved with honour by a government handout?—but the Government was getting more and more involved in the rescue effort. It wanted to avoid any backlash that would come if it was seen to have put off Laker Airways' collapse, but only until the 1982 summer holiday season had begun to pick up.

About the only concrete offer of help from the Government was made in November by Trade Secretary John Biffen. Laker had protested to the CAA that the fares Pan Am was charging were too low. They might be all right for an airline with Laker Airways' low costs, he argued, but they were obviously below breakeven for Pan Am. The Bermuda Agreement required that fares 'be established at the lowest level consistent with a high standard of safety and an adequate return to efficient airlines...' Pan Am was breaking that rule, claimed Laker, but the CAA turned the other way and approved the low, loss-making fares. British Airways and TWA kept quiet and matched them. John Biffen offered to overrule the CAA, but in order for him to be able to do so, Laker had to increase his fares to a higher base level. Laker refused. Other government schemes were dreamed up to help Laker during the run-up to Christmas, including one by Mrs Thatcher. But they were all deemed either to be impossible or to breach EEC rules or even British tax laws.

Meetings between one or other group of bankers, manufacturers and government officials reached crescendo pitch in mid-December, as the Exim Bank's deadline grew closer. On Tuesday, 15 December, there was a gathering of government officials from the Trade and Industry Departments, the Treasury, the Bank of England, and the CAA. Progress had been slow and there had been no blindingly simple plan to save Laker, so the government officials set their own deadline. Since holiday advance bookings are at their lowest level in December (in Laker's case down to £5·2 million in that month), if the company was to go broke, that was the best moment. The bankers and the rest were given until the end of the week to come up with a workable rescue plan, or Laker Airways' licences would be revoked by the CAA because the airline was in an inadequate financial condition to continue operating. It worked. By Thursday that week a tentative plan had been agreed that looked good enough for the British Government and the Bank of England to postpone the death sentence.

The plan was based on four main elements. Airbus Industrie would do what the West German and Austrian banks had wanted all along and would positively help Laker to find a buyer for the three Airbuses, but not until September 1982, at the end of the holiday season. Airbus Industrie would then have to put up the 25 per cent guarantee to cover part of the loss, the banks would shoulder the rest and Laker would be relieved in the meantime of the interest burden of $13 million a year on this loan. McDonnell Douglas and General Electric agreed to restructure the loan for the DC-10s. In principle what they offered was to convert the money that they had guaranteed (the first-loss guarantee), around $55 million, into preference shares. This would further reduce the repayment burden. In addition, there was to be an injection of cash as equity to improve the airline's appallingly stretched balance sheet. The CAA estimated that Laker needed an injection of £5 million to provide what it called some 'headroom'. And the two American manufacturers agreed to split this—£4 million to McDonnell Douglas, £1 million to General Electric. McDonnell Douglas understandably insisted that its offer was contingent on there being no material deterioration in Laker's already gloomy trading position.

It took until Christmas Eve to tidy up the loose ends to the point where the Bank of England was satisfied. That took some doing, because the CAA was warning internally that the low Pan Am fares were beginning to take a toll of Laker's Skytrain passengers. But right at the hour when most people are thinking about presents, tree lights and plum pudding, Samuel Montagu's Ian McIntosh was in the middle of a flurry of last-minute telexes and telephone calls to make sure that all was still well. The deal, in principle, held up and it was announced. Sir Freddie Laker emerged from a period of what had been, for him, monastic silence in the press. 'It is the best Christmas present of all time. We have secured our long-term future. We aren't going to lurch from one crisis to another.' The rescue, however, proved to be no more durable than one of those cheap, gaudy toys used to pad out children's Christmas stockings. It almost as quickly came apart.

Realization of what they had agreed to struck both McDonnell Douglas and General Electric over the Christmas break. Other airlines that were also their customers, some of them a great deal more valuable than Laker Airways, protested, just as Lufthansa had done to Airbus Industrie. The two manufacturers' offer to inject that £5 million as equity would have made them the majority owners of Laker. It was an impossible position. They also realized that the Americans would effectively be cross-guaranteeing Airbus

Industrie against any loss it might make on the 25 per cent first-loss guarantee from the planned sale of the three Airbuses in the coming September. The Euroconsortium would have had to make the payments to the banks in the first instance, but then it would have been able to claim the money back from Laker Airways, which would have been an American-owned company. The airline's finances by that time would be a great deal healthier, padded out with the injection of American share capital and the positive cash flow that the holiday season should by then have brought. It was expected that a positive cash balance of £12 million or so would have arisen in the month of August and that there would have been a positive cash flow (on a slightly more modest level) each month from then until December, even after allowing for the anticipated £7·5 million repayment to Airbus Industrie after the Airbus sale.

The first to break ranks was General Electric. It had been represented in London by Joe Galena, a lawyer from General Electric Credit Corporation. He was overruled by Brian Rowe, the head of the division that makes the engines. Rowe, a large and genial ex-Briton who began as an apprentice at De Havilland Engine Company, was as usual blunt and to the point. 'There is no way that we are putting equity into Laker,' he said. That meant that at best the original plan to inject £5 million of cash as equity was down to £4 million. General Electric also withdrew any thought that it had offered to convert into preference shares the £10 million arising from its portion of the guarantee it had been forced to give to Morgan Guaranty for its share of the DC-10 loan package.

McDonnell Douglas could not be so cavalier, given the state of the DC-10 programme. It left its offer of a cash injection of £4 million on the table, but as a loan instead of equity. 'There could be no question of McDonnell Douglas indirectly bailing out Airbus Industrie,' said the company's John Gentling, a vice-president of its finance corporation and its most frequent negotiator at the London talks. The banks that had actually lent the $46 million that McDonnell Douglas guaranteed were not pleased when they learned that the aircraft maker planned to renegotiate the loan in such a manner as to reduce their control over the way their money was used.

The pressure on the two American manufacturers to reverse what they had agreed was intense. Airlines in the United States were as unhappy as Lufthansa was with Airbus at the thought of major suppliers taking equity in a rival, especially when the rival was a foreign one that had given some of them so much trouble. The Exim Bank found itself in the same corner. 'We do not want to take stock [in Laker] because, frankly, Laker competes with Pan Am and TWA,' said Exim's chairman William Draper.

January produced yet more meetings, but this time to no good effect. The biggest problem was that Laker's trading position was deteriorating fast, thanks to Pan Am's low fares. 'You could see the load factor dropping off the edge, starting in November,' one of Laker's aides said later. The airline's chances had not been helped either by a series of rail strikes, which intermittently cut the convenient rail-link from London's Victoria Station to Gatwick. Skytrain's load factor had averaged 64 per cent during December and it had been anticipated that the percentage of seats filled would decline to 55 per cent or so in January. In the event, Laker's Skytrains in that month were flying barely 40 per cent full on average. The overdraft from Clydesdale Bank was rising fast, to pay wages and fuel bills, and increased from £6 million in December towards the airline's £9 million limit. In early January, to save money Laker sacked twenty-one of his captains and demoted ten more. The airline also hinted that the next two planned pay increases of 5 per cent each would have to go by the board.

The unhappy noises about Laker Airways' financial state were affecting the travel agents who did business with the company. Instead of handing over prepayments for holidays or tickets booked on the airline, they were hanging on to the money, waiting to see what would happen. If there was a choice, they were also booking their customers on another carrier or holiday company. Laker's day-to-day creditors were beginning to line up to be paid cash on the nail. The CAA reworked its figures: Laker Airways needed a £10 million cash injection, preferably as equity, if it was to survive satisfactorily.

At a meeting on Tuesday, 2 February 1982, the CAA was adamant that Laker needed £10 million, even though only £4 million was to be instantly available, from McDonnell Douglas. That company was growing increasingly unhappy at the prospect of immediately being dunned for a second tranche or instalment of cash almost before it had handed over the first. The CAA made it plain, too, that February's traffic on Laker Airways would be worse than January's. The second month of the year is traditionally the slackest month for travel and Laker was being undercut by the low fares of the established carriers.

That same day occurred one of the most bizarre episodes in the whole Laker story. Laker was on his way to New York—using Concorde, on a free pass of the sort given as a courtesy to all presidents of international airlines—to make some television advertisements. They were, incidentally, for Laker's version of first-class travel, the Regency class, and nothing to do with the 'forgotten man' he began Skytrain to serve. A reporter for Brenards News Agency, Steven Meller, collared Laker and asked him about the rescue. Laker, to put it politely, went off his head. 'All my financial worries are over,' he reckoned. 'A £36 million loan has been arranged from McDonnell Douglas which, with other bits and pieces, means new investment of up to £60 million. The future of the company is now very good. In fact we are in a better position than we have ever been.' If that were the case, then only Laker believed it. His claim was the last straw for the bankers back in London. They were furious at his irresponsibility. After making the commercials, in which he played the star (as usual), Laker and some of his staff celebrated in New York. His staff thought they were celebrating finalization of the rescue. Laker was told the truth when he returned to London on Thursday morning, having taken Skytrain back home on what he joked was his Cosh route (Concorde-out-Skytrain-home).

Enough was enough, was the message the Bank of England's industrial director, David Walker, had given the Midland Bank and its subsidiary at a private meeting on Wednesday. And that was the message they tried to impress on Laker that Thursday morning. He would not believe it, even after he had met with David Walker. What had sunk him, finally, was the Midland Bank's demand that he find another £5 million of equity to replace the money that the American manufacturers had withdrawn. The Midland Bank had also blocked Clydesdale from agreeing to Laker's request to increase the airline's overdraft beyond the £9 million by then already drawn. 'All along,' said Laker, 'they kept moving the goal posts'—an understandable feeling from his point of view. All along the financial hole into which his airline was sinking kept deepening. One factor which must have been in

Laker's mind was the risk of losing his licence from the CAA for trading while insolvent, which would have ended his chance of ever returning to the air.

Laker asked for, and received, agreement that nothing would be done by the bankers until first thing the following morning, Friday, 5 February. He began a frantic last-ditch effort to raise the £5 million.

However detached his view of reality might seem to have been two days earlier that week, one of his first actions on that Thursday afternoon suggests that he was well aware of what he was doing. He acquired an 'off-the-shelf' company from an agency. The company, called Brenpage, would be the vehicle to which he hoped to transfer the licences from Laker Leasing, the parallel company set up in Britain to hold the licences for his Jersey-domiciled airline, should Laker Airways actually go broke. Then Laker got to the telephone.

One of his calls went to Ian Sproat, a junior Minister in the Thatcher Government with responsibility for watching over aviation matters. There was no straightforward request for government aid. The call was ostensibly to let the Minister and the Government know what they had already been told through other channels: that Laker Airways, darling free-enterprise symbol of the Prime Minister, had failed. Nevertheless, once word reached Mrs Thatcher, she called a meeting of senior colleagues, including the Chancellor, and they went back over the ground in the faint hope that some new idea would strike them. It did not, and no help was forthcoming from that quarter. She was 'sad', but unbending.

Nobody he called had the kind of money he needed, or, if they had, was willing to put it up. One of the final shots was to call his old rival, Harry Goodman of Intasun. When they met in a fourth-floor suite of the Gatwick Hilton, Laker asked: did he want to buy something of Laker's operation that would produce the necessary cash? On offer were the two holiday companies, which were profitable concerns. No, said Goodman, who would clearly be able to pick up some of Laker's business more cheaply after a bankruptcy. And no, Goodman did not want to buy one or more of Laker Airways' Airbuses. Perhaps Goodman had in mind the way that Laker had treated him over the Miami holiday business, when he had turned Goodman's idea into a scheduled route. In any event, Laker's last throw of the dice had failed. After a board meeting, begun at three in the morning, there was nothing left to do but to telephone Samuel Montagu at eight o'clock on Friday and tell the Bank to call in the receiver. And Clydesdale Bank sent for Bill Mackey, a partner in the accounting firm of Ernst & Whiney.

There was an immediate attempt at a rescue after the event, by the Orion Royal Bank, the London-based subsidiary of the Royal Canadian Bank, which had been involved in the DC-10 loan to the tune of around $11 million. Orion, headed by former Tory Minister and four-minute-miler Christopher Chataway, had begun its planning for the rescue well before the receiver was called in. Pulling together all the information available from the many banks that had been poring over Laker's books, Orion reckoned that, even after allowing for the expected inflow of holiday deposits and the like, Laker Airways' cash deficit was likely to be £12 million, declining to a bottom position of £19 million by March. That, of course, did not allow for the way travel agents had begun withholding payments made to them for future bookings on Laker. In February, to cover the cash deficit and the monies needed to make the payments of principal and interest on the loans, Orion calculated that Laker needed an immediate injection of £35 million. That would have given the rescued company zero net worth. To allow it to operate adequately, it would also have needed a second tranche of at least £40 million as equity, to provide some working capital. It would also be necessary to persuade the bankers and equipment makers (and the Exim Bank) to agree to convert some of their loans to equity to reduce the payments burden from their present level of $48 million every six months. Orion reckoned that it had the promise of £35 million from a group of institutional investors, plus some rich people willing to take a gamble. But its plan foundered on the same rock as the earlier one: none of the major creditors was happy to take equity in Laker Airways.

Laker then turned to Roland 'Tiny' Rowland, who had waited until the dust had settled to telephone to say that if there was anything he could do, Laker was to call him. Rowland was the businessman whose activities former Tory Prime Minister Edward Heath had dubbed 'the unacceptable face of capitalism'. Under Thatcher's Government his company, Lonrho, had been denied permission to take over the House of Fraser, the company that owned Harrods department store in London. He still wanted Harrods and unkind people suggested that he was talking about rescuing Laker in order to persuade the Government to grant him official permission to acquire it.

In any event, this rescue failed, too, but the investigation by the official receiver and by accountants Peat Marwick on behalf of Mr Rowland's company, revealed a great deal of what had been going on with Laker's finances. All of the airline's 1979–80 profits, and almost all of its 1980–1 profits were the result of beneficial changes in the dollar-pound exchange rate. The *Sunday Times* reported that in 1980–1's unpublished accounts, £1·5 million of the £2·2 declared profit arose that way. The airline still only had the original £20,000 fully paid-up capital. In addition there had been a (perfectly legal) issue of £4·5 million of shares to the two stockholders, Laker and his former wife Joan, on a 90:10 split. The receiver found that bills totalling more than £20 million had not been paid by Laker Airways, which explains the growing unhappiness of many of its creditors. There were also suggestions that at least some of the money taken in as holiday deposits had been used to pay day-to-day bills rather than put into a protected bank account. All Laker's dreams of re-emerging speedily to cash in on the unprecedented wave of public sympathy dissolved. Nobody, not even Tiny Rowland, was going to be able to pick up the pieces. Much to Laker's mortification, the receiver began to sell off the company bit by bit in such a way that it could never be put back together again.

Among the first bits to go were the two profitable holiday companies, which between them raised £4·5 million. Arrowsmith went for £4 million to brewers Greenall Whitley (better known for its Warrington brand of vodka), and Laker Air Travel for £500,000 to Saga Holidays. The receiver may have got a better price even than it seemed at the time. A tremendous volume of holiday business that would otherwise have gone the way of these two companies had instantly been transferred by travel agents to other operators, including Harry Goodman's Intasun.

14 · Instant management—Laker-style

Paternalistic to a fault, Laker was also autocratic in the way he dealt with his staff. He made rapid decisions, whether or not they were in line with his previous policy, and having made up his mind he stuck to it rigidly—until he changed it again. He said that he would 'change his mind ten times a day if necessary . . . a man who does not change his mind does not think. Laker Airways is going to go on changing its mind, its fares and its products at any time that we feel that we have got it wrong.' This is all very well, but it made life hard for his employees, since the worst sin in his management book was to vacillate. That was worse than making the wrong decision. He ruled with an iron fist and handed out verbal lashings to those who, in his eyes, got things wrong. In a backhanded way he respected more those who shouted back, but, while he would admit it if he had been wrong about something, Laker sometimes found it hard to say sorry. He would sack people regularly, though most were promptly reinstated unless they had been caught cheating.

Very few of his staff could actually say 'No' to him and expect it to stick for any length of time. One of the four or five was Cliff Nunn, who had worked for Laker since the earliest days of BUA. Laker Airways' management structure was similar to that of a small charter line, which was just right for that sort of operator. While everybody at Laker Airways was skilled as an operator, there was a shortage of conventional management skills. And, because it was a private company, there were no outside directors to question what was going on. Everybody got on with whatever needed fixing, with no questions asked. A typical story concerns the very senior official from Whitehall who arrived at Laker's spartan Gatwick headquarters to find the finance director on his hands and knees with the Xerox machine spread about the floor as he tried to fix it. Financial control was one thing obviously missing, yet it was only when it was too late that the Midland Bank and its subsidiary, the Clydesdale Bank, imposed an outside financial controller to try to sort out the financial mess that the airline had been allowed to get into.

There are conflicting versions of Laker's management style. Usually, people recall stories about management planning being done on the back of an envelope, with most of the calculations being done in Laker's head. His friends say that is wrong, but Laker has himself to blame for most of this image; he delights in claiming to be able to get things right this way. His staff and advisors claim that a great deal of homework went into the preparation of cases for presentation to the CAA and the CAB, or into working out which routes should be applied for, and so on. Officials who had to listen to these cases universally reject this notion. Laker appeared at one hearing at the CAB to discuss whether or not IATA was a cartel that was against the public interest and whether, therefore, the United States should ban it. Laker made many wide and sweeping allegations, but when he was challenged (on technical points of order) by the then boss of Qantas, Sir Lenox Hewitt, who was appearing for the cartel, he could only bluster. Hewitt, who can be an annoyingly precise man when the mood takes him, said afterwards that he had the impression that nobody had ever stopped Laker in mid-flight and made him substantiate factually some of his wilder statements. Laker's intervention did not help the consumers' case against IATA.

On aircraft operating costs, it seems that Laker can do the sums on a small piece of paper and get them right. Expanding these numbers into a normal management plan seems to have been equally rudimentary. He would work out what revenue might be available from a 'reasonable', but largely estimated, passenger load on a particular route, subtract the aircraft operating cost and use the remainder to cover overheads and profit. This approach worked for BUA's South American routes, where there was profit to be made if the overheads were cut back to a reasonable level. But when it became clear that there might not be sufficient passengers to cover costs, as in the case of the Hong Kong route, it seemed that Laker simply increased what might be deemed to be 'reasonable'. His system was obviously far from effective when it came to accounting in general. This trait of ignoring formal accounting seems to have been with Laker from the beginning. When he was approached to sell his original companies, Air Charter and Aviation Traders, the buyers found that proper accounts had been sadly neglected. They bought the companies anyway.

Board meetings were distinctly *ad hoc* in nature. At one time, Laker Airways' public relations manager, Robin Flood, had a call from Ray Hankin, a travel journalist, who asked if it was true that the company was about to sell its profitable holiday subsidiary, Lord Brothers. Flood went to ask Laker, who was on the telephone discussing the matter. Having taken Flood's question, he yelled for the senior managers to gather and said: 'We have an offer, shall we sell?' The answer, gathered in less than a minute's discussion, was no. Laker told the person at the other end of the telephone and told Flood to call the journalist back with the same answer. Instant management, Laker-style.

Laker's most obvious skill was in managing aircraft and the people who flew and maintained them. His airline was always at the front of any development to reduce operating costs, such as calculating the minimum safe power needed for any take-off. Less load requires less power, which saves fuel. The aircraft were always kept polished because that paid off by saving a little fuel. Laker always managed to push the available range of his aircraft further than most other airlines. It has been no coincidence that his well-maintained aircraft were mostly taken up as they were made available by the receiver in what has, elsewhere, been a dead market for used airliners.

Laker's proudest and most justifiable claim to fame as an airline manager is that in thirty-four years in the flying business, no passenger was ever killed on one of his airliners.

There was no secret about Laker's strengths and weaknesses as a manager. And there was no secret about how much time the small team had wasted fighting useless causes for routes to Australia, the Far East and then around the world. The only surprising thing is that the banks took so long to appoint a financial controller—and when they did, it was too late to save the airline.

15 · Who abused whom?

Laker was a willing victim, but there is little doubt that both the British and American Governments made use of his existence. As the politicking over aviation policies evolved, so Laker and his Skytrain became a tool, useful first to one side and then the other. Skytrain's low fares—or, more accurately, the publicity that surrounded them—helped the Americans in their efforts to persuade the continental Europeans to allow increased competition on routes between their countries and the United States.

Inevitably, Laker himself became the centre of attention, and was flattered by it. He is a man who thrives on flattery, or perhaps on hero worship, and he was the recipient of a great deal of it in the first year or so after Skytrain began operating. But he is also vulnerable to the effects of flattery and has tended to believe his own publicity. He was positively fêted in the United States where he was the obvious focus that the administration needed for its efforts to promote the benefits of deregulation for the airlines. He was asked to testify to Congress and at CAB hearings, though sometimes he did not perform so well under cross-examination. As one of America's leading deregulators put it later: 'If Freddie had not existed we would have had to invent a substitute.'

Constant repetition of the line that he was the man who had revolutionized air travel and beaten governments appeared to make him feel invincible. He was told he stood no chance of getting all those other routes, to Hong Kong, Australia and into Europe, yet persisted in trying to prove people wrong, as he had with Skytrain. He also quite deliberately set out to take advantage of aircraft makers where and when he could, though some of his deals were not quite as good as he made them out to be. It is fair to say that after forty-odd years in the aviation business, he should have known just how massive the risks were that he was taking with his company.

It is also fair to say that he had totally inadequate advice from his bankers. He had been encouraged not only to overexpand but also to borrow in dollars for all of his deals. Given that the Mitsui loan ($58 million) and the loan led by Exim ($228 million) were already in dollars, the airline's balance sheet was dollar-heavy. Laker Airways' earnings were over 60 per cent in pounds sterling. Ideally there should have been a balance between the currencies involved in earnings and borrowings. Yet the loan from the Midland-led syndicate ($131 million) was also put into dollars. 'It was a bit silly,' Samuel Montagu's Ian McIntosh said later. To make matters worse, the bankers did not protect Laker against changes in the value of the pound against the dollar. When he took out these loans, ending with the Midland syndicate's loan on 15 February 1981, sterling was strong, running at $2.30 or more. Averaged out over all the loans, the dollar value of the pound when the loans were taken was $2.2445. At the time of the collapse, almost exactly one year later, sterling had sunk to around $1.80. This meant that there was an increase of 23 per cent in the number of pounds that had to be earned to repay these dollar-denominated debts. Over the ten-year life of the loans, assuming a constant $1.80 exchange rate from 1982 on, to meet the payments another £37·6 million was needed over and above what had been planned for.

Hindsight is an easy and sometimes dangerous tool to use when analysing a case like this. But it does seem surprising that no banker appeared to be sufficiently concerned about potential exchange losses at the time these loans were raised to do something about it. Hedging against currency changes by buying forward in the market is a normal part of financing international trade—or should be. This is, as McIntosh later conceded, a banking matter pure and simple. He feels that bankers shouldn't be pilloried for going along with Laker's view on whether or not his airline would get various routes or what load factor might be possible, which are matters for airline people to determine. But on giving loans all in dollars or not hedging against currency changes, he accepts that Laker's bankers bear a clear responsibility.

There is a surprising twist in this, involving the Thatcher Government, which suggests that Whitehall played a part in causing Laker's downfall. As already described, the Government subsidized the Airbus loan to keep the interest rate Laker Airways paid to a constant 10·2 per cent. This was to ensure that the Laker order for Airbuses, which British Aerospace took as its dowry when it rejoined the Airbus Industrie consortium, did not go awry. It is now clear that the British Government played a crucial role in seeing to it that this loan was denominated in dollars and not sterling.

It was not a special decision associated only with the Laker loan. The British Government insists that all Export Credit Guarantee finance raised in Britain for all Airbus sales is denominated in dollars. The Midland Bank had been instructed by the Treasury to raise the money in the Eurodollar market. Other airlines, with earnings in sterling, have asked to be allowed to borrow in pounds, but permission has always been refused. The reason is straightforward. Borrowing on the Eurodollar market reduces the amount of money deemed to have been borrowed by the public sector and so reduces the strain on Britain's balance of payments. The Government in Britain has a perennial problem with mounting public-sector borrowing to sustain the nationalized industries and to pay excessive wages in Britain's overlarge public sector. There was another side benefit. At the time the loan was made, the pound was strong and interest rates on sterling loans were higher than for dollars. That made the subsidy less if Laker's loan was in dollars. Fortunately for Whitehall (and unlike the Court Line case), there will be no official inquiry into the Laker Airways collapse, largely because there was no Government attempt at a rescue and no straightforward cash involvement in the airline's finances.

Was this decision, and the bankers' willingness to go along with it, justified in the light of what was then known? The collective wisdom was that the pound was going to stay strong. The Confederation of British Industry was bleating that the strong pound was going to kill off half of Britain's manufacturing industry because it made exports uncompetitive and at the same time imports more attractively priced. The theory that the petropound was going to remain strong was all the rage in Whitehall in early 1981. Yet at a ministerial meeting with Laker and his bankers to discuss the Airbus financing, a relatively junior civil servant asked

Laker what was proposed to protect the airline against currency shifts. Laker's inclination was not to worry since over the previous couple of years he had made large profits from the weakness of the dollar against the pound. Two-thirds of his earnings were in sterling, but the majority of his bills, especially on his massive borrowings, were denominated in dollars. Everything had been going his way. His response was a typically grand gesture towards his banker from Midland's Clydesdale subsidiary, and he told the meeting: 'That's what I asked him this morning.' The banker made reassuring noises that everything would be all right, incredible though that sounds now in the light of sterling's rapid decline in parity against the dollar, a decline that began just six months later.

Why, then, were the bankers so anxious to lend to Laker Airways? The Midland syndicate loan was, in fact, oversubscribed. The truth is that considerable doubts existed concerning the strain on Laker Airways' balance sheet. Morgan Guaranty refused point-blank to take part in the Midland-led syndicate for Laker's Airbuses, unless its stake was cross-guaranteed by General Electric. Dr Gernot Reiners, vice-president of Morgan Guaranty Trust, says: 'We told them [the makers] on Day One that Laker was not a bankable credit and we got 100% cover for our loan. We figured Laker had no staying power and we are not in the business of speculating in collateral values of aircraft.'

Laker Airways, in fact, looked gold-plated by comparison with some borrowers because of all that government involvement. The Mitsui loan for $58 million was guaranteed 100 per cent by the Japanese Government. The DC-10 loan of $228 million was backed by the US Government and the two manufacturers. Midland Bank had been pressured by the British Government to lead the $131 million Airbus loan, and that Government had then subsidized it. Moreover, Airbus Industrie (which is government-backed) was giving a first-loss guarantee. When bankers are protected from risk by such arrangements, their attitude, understandably, is: 'Why shouldn't we lend?' There is an argument to be made that it is naive to expect bankers to turn away what seems to be sure-fire business; in Laker's case it will be Governments, which means taxpayers, who will pay almost all the losses on these loans. The bankers will crawl away virtually unscathed. It was McDonnell Douglas and General Electric who were stung over the DC-10 loan ($46 million and $10 million respectively) and both companies wrote off their losses in their 1981 accounts. Airbus Industrie could lose some money too but, since it is a government-funded Eurocompany, that loss will be recouped from the three governments mainly concerned, those of West Germany, France and Britain. The only bank obviously to suffer at all is the Midland, through the £9 million overdraft, £5 million bond, and other debts its Clydesdale subsidiary allowed Laker's companies to run up. Nevertheless there is at least as powerful a case for arguing that bankers have a responsibility to watch over the interests of foolish borrowers. The Bank of England is deeply embarrassed by this aspect of the Laker collapse.

It was only later in 1981, when it was obvious that international aviation traffic was in a recession and Laker was clearly in trouble, that bankers began to wring their hands. Already suffering from Poland's rescheduling problems, the European banks suddenly had thrust upon them in mid-summer the example of Chase Manhattan's brutal treatment of Pan Am—the one-time giant of the international airline business. Not only did this bank force Pan Am to sell its hotels so that it could get its loans repaid intact, but Chase also led the move by all of Pan Am's bankers to end short-term lending to that airline. Otherwise, Pan Am's creditors feared, in the depressed 1981–2 aviation market they might end up stuck with unrecoverable debt except in the form of airliners that could only be sold at a huge loss. Laker Airways' fleet of 11 DC-10s, 3 A300s, and 4 1-11s had a book value at the end of March 1981 of £229 million. By that summer, when the German-speaking trio of banks proposed that these aircraft should be sold to pay off the debts, the fleet's market value was put at $325 million (at current exchange rates, or about three-quarters of book value). Bill Mackey, the receiver, reckoned in early 1982 that it might take two years to unload the fleet at a reasonable price. And in the meantime it would be necessary to pay storage charges and maintenance costs to keep the fleet in good condition, which is why he promptly set about leasing out, rather than selling, Laker's fleet.

Consortium banking is always difficult, but becomes almost impossible when there is trouble. The greater the number of countries that are involved (the Midland syndicate embraced banks from France, Canada, the United States and Britain as well as West

Germany and Austria), the greater the potential for disagreement. Each country has different priorities and methods of handling things. The German banks are in effect nationalized, for instance. There is the whole question concerning cross-directorships between the bankers and companies in their own countries, which may be rivals of the organization doing the borrowing. Add to that the fact that Laker was a weak borrower facing strong lenders, who demanded a contract that gave them a firm handle on what happened to their money, and the outcome (from today's vantage point) seems inevitable.

Cynics might note that Laker Airways was good enough to lend to, thanks to all that government backing, but that the bankers did not deem it creditworthy enough to be able to afford forward cover on its dollar loans, particularly the last one.

There is another unanswered question: why did Laker Airways never go public? The airline was declaring profits for every year of its existence, including the last set of accounts that were unpublished at the time of its collapse. Laker himself had always intended to go public at some stage. At the beginning of running his own airline, he said at one point that he was only waiting for the necessary three years of consecutive profits before doing so. And in 1980 he had issued those £4·5 million worth of paper shares— which would have made sense if he planned to go public, since it would have been reasonable for him to hope that it would make him a rich man, at least on paper. Yet his bank never encouraged this man. Could it be that his bankers had an inkling of what the prospectus would have to reveal—that there had been some inadequate accounting, as shown by the subsequent investigations of the receiver and Peat Marwick after the collapse?

Patriotism is something that Laker has in large measure. It is genuine. So it is sad that the knighthood that he is so proud of, that crowned his career, was the result of a blatantly political decision. After the Government had been defeated in the courts over Skytrain, which had then been adopted by the British Government as a weapon in the Bermuda 2 negotiations, the Secretary of State for Trade at the time, Edmund Dell, felt magnanimous towards Laker. He had even sent him a short note on the occasion of the first Skytrain flight wishing it and him well. (And had been upbraided by the Tory *Daily Mail* for writing only briefly!) Dell and his civil servants, led by John Steele, who is now director of transportation for the EEC, felt that some honour should go Laker's way. They recommended to Downing Street that Laker should have some lesser honour like a CBE in the 1978 Queen's Birthday Honours. Prime Minister Callaghan was by then already thinking about the coming election, which the Labour Party was going to have to fight on the defensive. Britain's economy was getting worse by the month. The rest of the Honours list was safe—and therefore boring. Adding a knighthood for Laker had more than one virtue: it not only brightened things up, since he was a popular winner; it stole the Tory Party's clothes. The Labour Party was lurching to the left and Callaghan, rightly, saw that this could cost his party the election. Laker's knighthood was no more than a weak smokescreen that did not help.

Subsidizing aircraft sales, in the way that Laker's aircraft purchases were all government-subsidized, is a foolish exercise. The failure of Laker Airways merely adds validity to that argument. All that governments are doing is to encourage airlines that cannot otherwise afford it to buy airliners that they often have no use for in any commercial sense. The fact that in most cases these airlines are government-owned doesn't alter this principle one jot.

What has been happening in the aircraft business parallels almost exactly what has already happened in shipbuilding. All sorts of plausible reasons are put forward to justify handing over large sums of subsidy. For military reasons it is necessary to have a strong shipbuilding industry. And for social and political reasons, which usually means winning votes in the interests of the ruling political party, the government of the day wishes to keep its manufacturing industry busy. But business has declined because demand for ships (or aircraft) has declined, and so larger and larger subsidies are needed to persuade people to take on more capacity than they need. Eventually market forces overtake government policies and the whole thing collapses like a pack of cards and turns politically sour. It happened worldwide in the shipbuilding industry in the period immediately after the OPEC price increase in 1973. And governments are still trying to reduce their shipbuilding industries to a more practical size in an orderly fashion, which means without losing too many votes in the process. The same thing could be about to happen to the aircraft business as it matures. People's desire to travel has not diminished but as fares rise (as they will do inevitably, which has nothing to do with the demise of Laker) their ability to afford air travel will not keep pace.

Lockheed dropped out of the civil aviation business in late 1981; McDonnell Douglas had received few orders for the DC-10 and it was losing money on the project; in 1981–2 Boeing was finding it hard to sell new aircraft, with or without government subsidy. The world's major aircraft makers were all unwilling to consider launching any new aircraft projects because they could not afford to raise the large sums of money that would be required. The attack on these export subsidies begun by the Reagan administration was striking sympathetic chords with the West Germans and the British. But in the meantime, of course, the handing out of subsidies continues, pushing the finances of airlines that are seduced by this cheap money closer to the wall.

16 · Business crises and private tragedies

With tragic irony, Laker suffered great personal blows at the time of both his major business crises. In 1965 Laker was considering leaving British United Airways to set up in business on his own: an airline that would include a tour company to be run by his eldest son, Kevin, then 17. Laker had always planned to pass on to Kevin an integrated Laker tour operation. But just after Laker had announced his resignation from BUA, Kevin was killed in a car crash. The Aston Martin he was driving (a detuned model) had been a gift from his father. Laker was devastated by Kevin's death. He grew further away from his first wife Joan, and their marriage broke up. Six weeks before he was due to leave BUA, he was involved in a row said to be over the sacking of an employee, and walked out. This was the last of several serious disagreements between Laker and BUA's chairman, Sir Myles Wyatt; they remained friends outside business.

The second crisis in Laker's personal life came just at the time of his bankruptcy and concerned his second son, Freddie junior, then four. Laker's third wife, American-born Patricia, took Freddie away from the family home at Chailey in West Sussex. Laker began a long courtroom battle to gain access to the boy, and the situation only began to improve at Christmas 1981, when Laker was allowed to spend some time with his son. Laker was vastly more distraught over the first of these tragedies, during the time of his departure from BUA. However, this second one meant that much of his time was spent in trips to Miami, where his son had been taken, and was a worrying distraction from the airline and its impending collapse.

17 · What did Laker achieve?

A clear achievement of Laker and his Skytrain, for which all air travellers on the North Atlantic had cause to be grateful between 1977 and 1981, was to expose IATA for the cartel that its international fare-fixing has always made it. As soon as it became clear in June 1977 that Skytrain was going to be designated for London–New York, the established carriers on the North Atlantic got together to decide how best to block its chances. It took three lengthy meetings at IATA's headquarters in Geneva to come up with an agreement for a package of fares to use against Skytrain. The three major airlines on the London–New York route, Pan Am, TWA and BA, with BCal as an additional, minor, carrier, had quite different ideas on the best way to deal with Skytrain. Complicating matters, there were thirty-seven other airlines involved in the discussions because they flew between other points across the North Atlantic and would be affected by the outcome. Many details of IATA's normally confidential deliberations were exposed, thanks to Laker's sharp American lawyer, Bob Beckman. He used the US Freedom of Information Act to extract everything Pan Am had filed with the CAB in Washington when it applied for approval for its Skytrain-rival fares. Included was a copy of the three sets of IATA minutes.

The first session which ran from 11–15 July showed clearly what was going on and the split that existed among the three main carriers involved. All three, and many of the others too, wanted to take advantage of the growing willingness of the American and British Governments to approve low fares for scheduled carriers. The airlines' primary concern for some time had been competition from charter operators, and the fares they considered at the meetings were aimed at them at least as much as against Skytrain. Charters in 1977 carried over 28 per cent of all air passengers across the North Atlantic from all points in Europe. Over one-third of those charter passengers were carried on charter flights operated by scheduled airlines that were members of IATA. So charter flights and their competitive fares were a major preoccupation for the cartel; Skytrain was a new and unproven threat. Competing with these two different non-IATA competitors required different rival fare types from the scheduled carriers. The problem for the big three was that while they accepted in principle that there was a difference, they could not agree on the details. Competing with charters, according to BA, required a low fare coupled with an advance-booking period of 21 or 30 days, and a required minimum length of stay. The airline already had APEX fares of this sort, but wanted to improve upon them (i.e., make them cheaper) so that they would also compete against Skytrain. BA called its offering to the cartel Super APEX. Pan Am called its idea Budget fare; it was intended to compete head-on against both charter and Skytrain. In what seemed a sensible idea, Budget fares required passengers to book at least 21 days in advance for travel in a particular week; the airline would later choose a day in that week with low bookings and then notify Budget fare passengers when they would be allowed to fly. Its disadvantage to the passengers was that they could not know precisely when to reserve hotels and other arrangements. For the airline it more than doubled the cost of clerking and computer time needed to handle an already low-profit-margin passenger. TWA's idea was simple and aimed directly at Skytrain: Standby fares. At fares barely higher than Laker's Skytrain, these were to be booked as available on the day of travel and, once booked, to be indistinguishable from a much more expensive standard economy ticket. This particular fare, Pan Am confessed to the CAB later in July, 'except as a competitive response to Laker, could not be justified on economic grounds'.

IATA's members had expected at first that Skytrain would be treated as a special kind of charter service and, therefore, that they would be able to leave it to the American charter to create direct competition. For a time Transamerica said it was going to run no-frills, instant-booking copies of Skytrain, called Skybus, but to points in continental Europe. And more than one IATA member (KLM and Sabena included) threatened to do the same if their traffic was seriously affected. Hence the airlines' confusion as it became clear that Skytrain had become a rival scheduled service.

While charter operators and their competitive fares were the item uppermost in the minds of the cartel, there can be no doubt that its members were also keen to see off Skytrain, if that was possible. And if Skytrain should disappear rapidly, a constant cry from many carriers was that they then wanted an immediate 'get-out' clause to allow them to drop the low fares that were being discussed. The aviation authorities in Britain and the United States admitted soon after this that they would have been powerless to prevent this blatant piece of anti-competitive behaviour from taking place.

The IATA minutes do not identify which member is being reported, but there are clues. With the carrier most likely concerned nominated in brackets, the following series of extracts from the first of the three anti-Skytrain meetings of the cartel gives a flavour of what was going on.

[Pan American] believed full and frank discussion on the problems arising from the Skytrain service introduction would result in an agreement which would satisfy both the needs of the designated carriers on the route [London-New York] and the desire of other carriers to protect the entire North Atlantic market.... [Pan Am's] proposal was a limited response at the outset, and if agreeable to the traffic conference would be introduced on the basis of a very carefully limited number of seats in order to keep the size of the problem in perspective.

[TWA] estimated that 26 per cent of its present [London–New York] traffic could be affected by the introduction of a Skytrain service. Its proposal was similar to Skytrain with fares 10 per cent higher, but would include all amenities and be commissionable [to travel agents]. Operating it between Kennedy and Heathrow would make it more convenient for passengers.

[British Airways] said if Skytrain were the only problem facing North Atlantic carriers any fare introduced on scheduled services to match it was potentially more damaging than the service itself; experience in other parts of the the world has demonstrated the dilutionary effects of standby fares. [BA] also wanted to introduce part-charter fares [i.e., to carry charter

passengers at the back of otherwise normal scheduled services].
IATA might not at any other time be able to seize the changed
attitudes of governments to low fares on scheduled services,
since airlines would not later have a strong enough case for
persuading governments to even the charter/schedule balance.

The debate about the effect on other North Atlantic routes of
Skytrain and the fares being devised to compete with it on the
London–New York route took up a great deal of time. A typical
reaction came from a continental European carrier that said it
would 'willingly co-operate' with the big three if they were obliged
to take action to compete with Skytrain. However, this carrier
'hoped that the proponents would not take advantage of the
situation to discuss other market competitive fares. . . . use of
Skytrain-type fares was highly objectionable.' Pan Am's original
idea was that the competitive fares would be available on an either/
or basis; the carriers would have to choose which one they would
offer, though they could later switch if one proved to be better than
the others. There also had to be either a strict time limitation on
when these fares were to be available—one carrier suggested just
to March 1978—or a get-out. One airline said it 'would require an
escape clause to allow a carrier to cancel any agreement with due
notice if this were found necessary', which meant if Skytrain failed
to stay the course. Strict control of how many cheap seats were to
be made available was also a hot topic at the second anti-Skytrain
meeting of the cartel on 22 July. Laker by this time was to be
allowed to offer 345 seats each way each day on a DC-10, with no
limitations, such as cutting back winter capacity to Boeing 707
levels. So Pan Am's proposal was that the three majors should each
be allowed to sell at the rate of 75 cheap seats a day each way,
averaged over a week, and the three carriers with fifth-freedom
rights London–New York (Air India, Iran Air and El Al), 40 seats
a day each way, again averaged over the week. Averaging would
allow airlines to fill up particularly empty flights and to save up
cheap seats when flights were full. The calculation also just
happened to produce 345 cheap seats a day each way between the
scheduled carriers. Between them and Skytrain, around one-
quarter of the seats available on scheduled services between
London and New York were to be offered at low-cost fares.
At the second session it became clear that for many IATA

members the real problem was not so much Laker's Skytrain as the APEX fare that was being proposed by BA. The cartel had long resisted this type of low fare and, while it was initially being proposed strictly for the North Atlantic, there was a fear that it would spread. (It did.) One member made it clear that Standby/ Budget fares would be available for only a very limited capacity on the North Atlantic. APEX fares would affect normal fare traffic and 'was not intended to respond to the immediate problem of the Skytrain service'.

At the third session of the cartel, on 10–12 August, the subject of Laker and his Skytrain or charters was, according to the minutes, barely mentioned at all. The airlines were more concerned about getting their own particular fare type included in an agreement, or of trying to find some way to agree a package. IATA's rules at that time required that votes on items such as fares be unanimous. There are also complex formulae that relate fares on similar routes, so that a second tier of slightly higher fares, based on the London– New York fare, would normally be fixed for places like Amsterdam and Frankfurt to New York, and a third still higher fare tier for places further away, and so on. The Lufthansa representative made it clear that the fears of the big three about London–New York had gone too far and were threatening to affect his airline's profits from Germany to the United States. 'The over-reaction [to Skytrain] seen at the beginning of the traffic conference has now considerably worsened.' The German airline did not believe it was necessary to reduce fare levels right across Europe in order to combat Skytrain. There was, however, general anxiety to come to some agreement. The cartel had been unable to come up with a fully agreed fare package for the North Atlantic since 1973, when competition from charters had intensified and the scheduled carriers had joined in and operated their own charter flights to retain market share. There was already only a limited agreement. And agreement on the North Atlantic fares pact was essential to the cartel since it affected so many other international air routes that pass from the New World through Europe to the Middle East, Africa or Asia.

The biggest trouble maker in this effort to achieve agreement was BA, which was insisting on getting agreement that it could operate Super APEX fares to the United States. It had been trying for years to wangle this and had always been resisted by other members of the cartel as much as by governments. The airline repeated again and again at Geneva its line that governments were vulnerable to such a proposal. What BA really meant was that it had never had such a chance of bullying this type of low fare through IATA. At the final session on anti-Skytrain fares, one airline said that the only advantage of being able to agree to the various fares being proposed was that they would then be tied strictly to capacity controls that would match cheap seats on IATA carriers to the capacity Laker was to offer. To help achieve unanimity, BA withdrew its other dream of getting part-charter on scheduled services, and as a result all the other carriers' objections were whittled away. At the end just one remained, from the Greek carrier Olympic, which had wanted massive cuts in fares from Greece to the United States. This was to prevent people discovering that it was cheaper to buy a ticket to London and a separate cheapie from London to New York than to fly direct from Athens. In the end this airline, too, caved in before the steamroller of the big three.

The package they agreed to was covered by a 'limited agreement', which was an agreement in name only. Any carrier could, by giving notice, ignore any of the provisions if the need (or the whim) arose. And the big three agreed to disagree and to file their own versions of competitive fares: Budget, Standby, and Super APEX. And then they, together with Air India, Iran Air, and El Al, filed to offer all three fares. The CAB agreed instantly to the Standby fare, since it was in straightforward competition with Laker. It was selling at marginal prices seats that would otherwise go unsold and would therefore be wasted. But the CAB's new chairman, Professor Kahn, was less keen on the Budget and Super APEX fares since they were directly aimed at charter operators and not Skytrain. But despite his misgivings, and after some discreet prodding from the White House, the Budget fare and Standby fare were approved. The CAB rejected BA's Super APEX fare, though the White House later overturned that. Britain's CAA felt that it had no choice but to accept whatever was proposed as anti-Skytrain fares, for fear that at this late stage the Americans might revoke Laker's licence to operate Skytrain.

What the airlines did in Geneva—and have done many times before and since—is against the laws relating to business of the United States, the EEC, Britain, West Germany and almost every other industrialized country. The difference is that it is sanctioned by governments for the airlines and for shipping, too. However blatant the cartel may have been in fixing things so that it made life convenient for the airlines, it was deemed to be easier to allow the airlines to get on with it than for fare-fixing to be a matter for civil servants. To be sure, some governments laid down guidelines for their national airlines. For example, Spain and Belgium insisted on fares as low as possible, when they could persuade the rest of IATA to agree, as a way of attracting passengers or tourists to come to their countries and spend hard currency. (Until recently the Belgian Government never worried about the massive losses of national carrier, Sabena.)

The members of the cartel have competed only when they absolutely had to—and that has meant when there has been competition from non-members. For the most part, since the Second World War, that competition has come from charter operators. As already pointed out, in order to compete the IATA airlines had gone into the charter business too; on the North Atlantic, Pan Am was for a while the biggest charter operator of all. A detailed study of air fares by the International Civil Aviation Organization (an agency of the United Nations) showed that in 1970–3 the lowest fares were offered where charter competition was hottest. In itself this is not surprising, but given governments' willingness—and in the case of countries like West Germany, positive encouragement—for the cartel to carve up the market, it is no surprise either that international air fares in general stayed so high. In 1977, Laker provided no more than another example of this phenomenon, except that, with the help of his advisors, he publicized what was going on within IATA in such a way that its clear anti-consumerist stance could not be ignored.

Even so, action to curb the cartel only occurred because of the coincidental timing of the radical change in the United States Government's aviation policy. Without Jimmy Carter in the White House and Alfred Kahn at the CAB, it is unlikely that the ensuing attack on the cartel would have even begun, with or without Laker and his exposure of IATA's warts. The first move by the United States against IATA was to end the anti-trust immunity granted to its international carriers. No longer would it be tolerated for an American airline to take part in any of IATA's activities. Nonsensically, this also included the wholly good and useful work the organization did as a trade association on matters such as safety standards, negotiating international air lanes over unfriendly countries and anti-hijacking procedures. Losing the annual dues from major airlines like Pan Am and TWA, as well as the disruption caused to the cartelization of air fares, prompted the member airlines to act. There had in any case already been a tiny swell of concern that the organization was not adapting to a changed world. This had begun in the period after the OPEC oil price rise and had been led by the two British state-owned airlines, BEA and BOAC, later merged to form BA. Surprising as it may seem, the British have always been more in favour of a small amount of competition than most of the international carriers.

Despite the unhappiness of the smaller airlines in regions like the Middle East and Africa, who could not see why 'their' cartel was being torn apart to suit the major airlines that flew the North Atlantic, IATA split itself in two. The deed was organized by the major airlines, mostly for their own benefit, and was steamrollered through at a special annual general meeting of the organization in Montreal in 1978. In the hope that it might mollify the Americans, the trade association side of IATA was to be separated from the cartelized traffic conferences. At the same time, the way these conferences worked was altered so that the wishes of the major airlines could not be blocked by a single vote from one of the smaller fry. Airlines flying from end to end of a particular market (usually the larger ones) were to be able to fix fares, capacity rules and the rest to cut out the airlines in the middle (mostly the smaller ones) in order to stop them poaching traffic. Laker's Skytrain was the cause of the upheaval, and was reviled in almost every speech and intervention at the Montreal special annual meeting, but its existence and market effect had very little to do with the framing of the actual detailed changes. At the same time, IATA got itself organized to reverse the United States' block on American carriers' participation in its trade association activities.

Through IATA, the airlines were organized to lean on their governments to protest in Washington about the way the Americans were imposing their domestic policies on the rest of the world. This is a common American trick and a wholly objectionable interference with other countries' sovereignty. The airlines, through their governments, found a ready ally in the US State Department, and the anti-IATA policy was toned down. In the end, United States airlines were prevented only from taking part in traffic conferences that affected the North Atlantic routes. If Carter had been re-elected for a second term as President, that provision might have become law. But almost immediately the Reagan administration took over in Washington, the big American airlines began to lobby for even greater relaxation of the anti-IATA stance. What became known as the 'Gang of Five' (Pan Am, TWA, Braniff, Northwest Orient and the freight carrier, Flying Tiger) called for different priorities. Instead of the drive by the CAB for more competition on international routes—more airlines flying between more cities and fares as low as possible—the five wanted a return to protection. They claimed the Carter policies had resulted in a loss of market share for United States carriers. And the Reagan administration, true to the Republican philosophy of pleasing big business rather than encouraging free enterprise, agreed. Coincidentally, just after Laker's demise, IATA moved back into favour with Washington. The pendulum had swung back the other way—and in more ways than one.

The mere existence of Laker Airways on the North Atlantic—by this time operating to New York, Los Angeles and to two airports in Florida—was regarded as a kind of talisman by the Reagan administration. The simple presence of a service called Skytrain, Washington felt, would keep the rest honest and stop air fares from rising faster than they otherwise might. That ignored the major change that was occurring in Laker's own policies. As his airline sank deeper and deeper into the financial mire, so he became more interested in pushing up fares. His airline was the leader in increasing fares in early 1981; that the increase did not stick and he had to retreat does not alter that fact. Later in the year, Laker almost gave in and joined the cartel. Detailed special negotiations were going on in Miami concerning North Atlantic air fares. These negotiations also played a part in parallel talks between the United States Government and the organization representing the Western European countries' aviation interests (ECAC), which included the reinstatement of IATA. That he did not join the 'enemy' was dictated more by the fees that would have been demanded by IATA than by his principles. Laker simply could not afford to pay, yet the talks were vital to his future. There was a technical reason why he was excluded, too, though it could have been overcome if the British Government had pressed the point. The American airlines taking part, Pan Am and TWA, had been given anti-trust immunity to discuss fares, but only with members of IATA. Laker was not a member of IATA, and therefore had to be kept out of the talks. So the British Government representative at these negotiations briefed Laker Airways' staff at the end of each session and took back to the next session that airline's views.

Rumours abound that there might have been some collusion among the major scheduled airlines on the North Atlantic concerning the fare cutting that occurred in November 1981. Laker Airways had grown to be a sizeable carrier on the North Atlantic. It was number four in terms of passengers carried in 1981, behind TWA, BA and Pan Am, but ahead of the likes of Lufthansa and Air France. His Skytrain operation had in the end been tolerated—the other scheduled carriers had little choice in reality—provided it kept to the lower end of the market. But then, in the autumn of 1981, Laker had announced that he wanted to go upmarket to include the Regency class, which amounted to a first-class service with all the trimmings. That took him into head-on competition in the prime, high-yield market of the big three on the Britain–United States routes. It was Pan Am that led the attack, with its massive fare cuts of up to 59 per cent from 1 November 1981. BA and TWA needed no second invitation and followed suit. All three were losing money hand over fist and yet felt able to cut prices to below break-even point, even for a 100 per cent full aircraft. The low fares had an effect on Skytrain's loads that all the earlier attempts by the big three to devise competitive fares had failed to achieve.

Laker's traffic was halved and this was the final straw that pushed his airline over the edge. There have been accusations that there had been deliberately predatory pricing, but there is absolutely no proof of any sort. Pan Am had rejoined the IATA trade association in early 1981, but was still not a member of the normal cartelized traffic conferences. However, while he would not be identified in any way, one boss of a continental European airline said with a grin, when asked if there had been collusion against Laker: 'I wouldn't be surprised, would you?'

By the time it collapsed, Laker Airways had developed into a major force in the North Atlantic market. Shared between its routes from Gatwick, Manchester and Prestwick to New York, Los Angeles, Miami and Tampa, in 1981 it had 5·3 per cent of the total North Atlantic market—that is, of all the passenger traffic between the whole of Western Europe and all two dozen gateway airports available to foreign airlines within the United States. In itself that share was a remarkable achievement, and it was up from 4·7 per cent in 1980, partly thanks to Laker Airways' having added the Tampa route in the meantime. It was no wonder that the major airlines had to take notice of what plans Laker had for fares on his services. They waited in early 1981 to see what he was going to file before they put in for their own fare increases with the British and American Governments. And then they followed his lead like sheep—first raising the fares considerably, then withdrawing, finally raising them only a little. This illustrated the first law of airline marketing: do what the other fellow does exactly and without question, for fear of losing market share, and all this only if you cannot agree privately beforehand what the increases should be.

Laker Airways' market share on its prime routes is even more impressive. In 1981, between New York and Britain, Laker had a 15 per cent market share, a 31 per cent share on the routes to Los Angeles and 32 per cent of the routes to Miami. However, these shares need to be put into some perspective. They are derived numbers and so are best estimates based on what is known of the detailed figures for the major airlines. The total figures for passenger travel are known from government sources. The gap is 'adjusted' for what is known about smaller carriers' traffic on the routes and Laker's share is estimated from the remainder. One of the side-effects of Laker's arrival on the international market is that organizations like IATA grew suddenly coy about releasing statistics that previously had been available in great detail. Recently there has had to be a lot of 'guesstimating', based on available information. These figures concerning Laker Airways are, however, sufficiently realistic to be certain that Laker was not, in fact, over-stretched on the North Atlantic. The market share achieved was more or less in line with the capacity that Laker Airways was offering. The second law of international airline marketing (where governments limit the number of carriers that can fly a route and how much capacity may be offered) is that each airline normally gets passengers in direct proportion to the number of seats it offers. Hence the anxiety of government officials to keep tabs on the capacity that other countries' airlines can offer to their home airports. The rule only breaks down if there is a large-scale public debate about the safety of a particular carrier, or if its cabin service is found to be dramatically worse than its rivals' or, more rarely, much better. (The cartel tries to make sure that the latter deviation cannot happen.)

On the routes to New York, Laker Airways had a 13 per cent share of the total capacity on offer and so was slightly ahead of the race in that market with a 15 per cent share of passengers. But it was offering 32 per cent of the capacity to Los Angeles and so was marginally behind in that market. This perpetuated the image of Laker's Skytrain in these two markets that had existed from the beginning—that it was a cheap way to travel but was full of unwashed backpackers. This might have been an advantage in America's north-east, since people there are always on the lookout for a bargain. But in California people think of themselves as more sophisticated and demand a little luxury.

So there were a lot of people willing to fly on Skytrain. The big question is whether this proves, or disproves, Laker's claim that he was going to serve the 'forgotten man', a class of passengers that the existing airlines (scheduled or charter) did not serve adequately. Or was this just a brilliant marketing ploy to use against governments in order to get round the very limiting rules for charter services in the early 1970s? Laker's friends and employees maintain still that there was such a class of passenger and the proof lies in the number of passengers carried on the routes Laker was allowed to fly. Nobody else in the business believes the claim. As one senior British civil servant described it, having had to listen to it many times, Laker Airways' market justification went like this: 'There is no need to do surveys or projections, since Laker sets the market. Passengers go where the fares are cut. Laker Airways suggests where they will take themselves on holiday through pricing.' And in a pure holiday market, complete with package tours, there is undoubtedly something in this. It also worked to some extent on the routes to Florida as long as there was a sufficiently large differential between sterling and the dollar to make American sun look cheaper than Mediterranean sun. For the most part, however, the figures do not support the claim at all.

Laker's people have never publicly put forward a convincing case. The American CAB listened to the broad claims but they were never given detailed analyses. Because it was in favour of more competition, and therefore of Laker, it refrained from any public wrist slapping, though its kindest private judgment was a shrug of the shoulders. Britain's CAA was not as polite. The airline's economic case when applying for the London–Hong Kong route, which turned on there being lots of 'forgotten people' waiting to fly that route, was flatly rejected by the CAA. Laker's case was, says the Authority's Ray Colegate, 'very childish'. The judgment in this case spelled out the CAA's objections:

> Laker assumed that these 'forgotten' men and women constituted a large potential demand, but offered no convincing evidence as to its size. Indeed the starting point for Laker Airways' passenger forecast seems to be the number of passengers it would need to carry in order to achieve a viable service rather than any serious quantitative calculation of what demand might be, with the result that the final forecasts of total market size and rates of growth exceed any reasonable expectation by a very wide margin.

That this judgment was overturned by Trade Secretary John Nott does not affect its validity; the reversal was a piece of Tory politics.

The case for the 'forgotten people' is best examined in relation to the North Atlantic economy-fare market during the period surrounding Skytrain's introduction. What the figures show very convincingly is that since 1977, there has been a small but steady decline in the number of full-fare economy passengers, i.e., those on middle-sized, but largely untrammelled expense accounts. This share of the total number of passengers who flew the North Atlantic has been between 23 per cent and a peak of 25·8 per cent in 1977 for the scheduled carriers, and has since dropped back to around 20 per cent. As already discussed the dramatic change has been in the number of charter passengers. Some of these transferred to Skytrain. But a larger share switched to normal scheduled flights, using reduced fares. The proportion on scheduled carriers of passengers using discount fares of one sort or another, such as the Super APEX fare that BA pushed so hard for, increased from 51–3 per cent in the early 1970s (with a low of 49 per cent in 1977) to 64–5 per cent in 1980–1.

The total number of passengers crossing the North Atlantic grew overall during the period. During the 1970s, growth rates in the aviation market were much more volatile than in earlier periods and the North Atlantic was hit hardest by these vagaries because it is a relatively mature market. Nevertheless the trend is clear. Early in the decade, IATA members lost passengers on both charter services and normal scheduled flights. Later in the decade, as passengers were attracted away from charter operators by discount fares on the established carriers, the proportion taken by charters was dropping by a quarter or more a year. This decline continued even in years when there was overall growth in the market. As the CAA puts it:

> The rate of traffic growth on the North Atlantic does not suggest the generation [by Skytrain] of any significant additional traffic: the rate of growth in the period after the introduction of Skytrain was consistent with that of the two previous years, taking scheduled and charter together, and there was no dramatic increase.

This is a nebulous area and Laker fans will dispute hotly that his innovation of an instant-booking, walk-on charter service called Skytrain had no discernible effect on the market's size. But that is the case, however hard it may be to convince those who prefer to believe the mythology surrounding Laker, which is much more glamorous than ploughing through masses of dry statistics. Much the same sort of post-recession travel rebound occurred in 1977–8 on domestic routes in the United States as on the North Atlantic. And that was the time when the apostles for deregulation were preaching their fervent message at the CAB. Low fares of one sort or another were all the rage for America's domestic routes and by the second half of 1978 about one in three passengers on scheduled services there used one or other of the many cut-price offers. (Remember that fares in the United States are already low by world standards.) In the second half of 1977, around one in four scheduled passengers had used cheap fares. It is impossible to be precise, as there is no way of calculating how many people travelled using a cheap fare who would otherwise have stayed at home (Laker's 'forgotten people'), or how many switched to low fares from normal and more expensive ones. But it has been estimated by analysts that of the 15 per cent growth in 1978, less than a quarter can be accounted for by low fares.

Certainly, IATA's economists doubted that low fares had much to do with the 1978 traffic boom. That year, world-wide, there was a 19 per cent increase in scheduled traffic and a 12 per cent drop in charters. On the North Atlantic, there was a marked discrepancy between the growth rates in each direction. The increase of over 19 per cent in traffic arising in Europe contrasted with an 8 per cent increase in US passengers. The difference is largely a result of changes in the relative strengths of the pound and dollar. 'The results suggest that the new low fares produced very little traffic generation,' said IATA's economists in the autumn of 1978.

What Laker did for British civil aviation policy is perhaps best illustrated by what happened as soon as he had gone broke. In the time since Skytrain started in 1977, Laker Airways grew to take a major slice of the market with the United States. This helped restore the balance of aviation trade between the two countries so that it was nearly 50:50, instead of the 69:31 split favouring the USA when Britain denounced the Bermuda Agreement in 1976. It is hard to see how BA and BCal would have achieved that increase in Britain's share unaided, however restrictive a treaty the British Government had been able to wheedle. BA's costs are so high that it cannot afford to try to increase its share in any market. Each extra flight it puts on adds to its losses. And BCal is happiest when it is given protection by government and preferably monopoly routes. It earlier failed to cope with either New York or Los Angeles, though it moved back onto the latter route when Laker Airways went bankrupt, in an effort to pick up a slice of Laker's market share. Because he had built up an excess of capacity to fly around the world, Laker had spare aircraft that had to be used somewhere. On the principle that market share is dictated by the capacity offered, Laker became useful to Britain's obtaining a half share. He was also an energetic publicist. Britain now has no carrier willing or clearly able to pick up such extra work and make a go of things. To prevent a backsliding of the overall British market share so painfully won following the renegotiation of the Bermuda 2 Agreement, the British Government told the Americans that the treaty would no longer be interpreted as casually as it had been. The first sign is that no extra gateway will be added between the two countries.

A sad commentary on the swing away from encouraging competition on the international air routes was that Britain's change of heart found sympathetic ears in Washington. There was a sharp reversal of views on deregulation immediately after the Reagan administration took office. However, for all the

admiration in Washington for what Laker stood for, this U-turn
would have happened whether or not his airline went broke. Laker
was not and has never been a deciding factor in United States'
international aviation policy. Because of his abiding respect for
Laker, Professor Alfred Kahn is reluctant to say so, but he believes
that almost everything that happened on the North Atlantic would
have happened anyway. While wishing it was otherwise, Kahn's
assessment is that most of the changes in the latter part of the 1970s
arose either from the scheduled carriers' concerns about
competition with charter operators, or from the structural changes
brought about by United States' policy. The biggest factor was the
change in the nature of American bilateral agreements, beginning
with those with small countries like Belgium and the Netherlands,
and then with West Germany. Laker was extremely useful to the
Americans in 1977–8 because of the large amounts of good
publicity that surrounded him, and therefore the virtues of cheap
air fares. He was the little-man-made-good, an out-and-out
entrepreneur whose appeal to the American public matched that of
motherhood and apple pie. And he had beaten the big, bad
brigades at their own game. 'They', meaning governments, had
tried to stop him, but he had won in court. Then the major airlines
had been caught red-handed trying to kill off Skytrain and with it—
in the public's mind—easy-to-use low air fares. The Carter
administration was pushing the idea that low air fares were good
for the American people, and that they had been provided courtesy
of Jimmy Carter; Laker was a godsend.

In just one respect Laker did have a specific effect on American
international aviation: Standby fares. They had been tried on
domestic routes, but it was only in response to Skytrain that the
international carriers considered offering very low fares free of an
advance booking period and not tied to some other artificial
requirement, such as an often fictitious group membership.

More recently, Kahn has expressed concern about whether the
American-led increase in competition in international aviation can
be sustained permanently. International aviation is never going to
be a free market. Governments are inevitably going to be involved
in something as inherently dangerous as allowing other countries'
airliners to fly over their territory. And there are obvious foreign
policy considerations, too. Kahn considers that:

It may still happen that the established carriers' new policy [i.e., since 1977] of quickly meeting competitive fares on the nose, and perhaps their superior staying power from a more diverse route structure, plus subsidies for some international carriers, might continue to drive out newcomers. This is especially the case where they meet special fares selectively, the more so since most passengers still prefer to travel by the old established carriers if they can afford to.

Without wishing for governments to prevent existing carriers from competing with newcomers, Kahn wonders whether they might consider putting a limit on the fare increases that the surviving carrier can introduce for a period after the competitor leaves a market or has been driven out of business. 'I never claimed competition worked perfectly,' Kahn reminds one.

Inevitably, the collapse of Laker Airways in early 1982 led to idle speculation in the airline business: suppose Laker had stuck to what he knew best? When he started Laker Airways back in 1966, he had made it clear that his idea was to keep the business small, with no more than ten aircraft. He was an expert at finding open niches in the charter and holiday markets. And his original Skytrain idea worked. The New York market was an obvious one, since it was the largest single international route—around one-quarter of all international travel. It became profitable almost immediately, as Laker claimed it was from the first day. Los Angeles took over a year to get into the black. But if he had stuck to these two routes and had not purchased enough equipment to run Skytrain services all over the globe, it is likely that he would have still been in business. He was a rarity in the civil aviation business in any case. Until his last year, he had declared a profit in every other one of the thirty-four years that he had run an aviation company (leaving aside the fact that there had been some lax accounting towards the end of Laker Airways). But that was not enough for Sir Frederick Alfred Laker.

Epilogue · A marvellous catalyst

Weep no tears for Freddie Laker. He knew from the start that he risked going broke—and made no secret of it. He even said just after receiving the final court verdict on Skytrain that 'a day like today almost makes it worthwhile going bankrupt.' He was a rarity in Britain: a real live entrepreneur who made a success of things in a big way (until he failed, in a similarly big way) and joyously celebrated his success. It was no surprise that the British public warmed to him.

He thought the risk was worth taking. The Laker story has been one of a rank outsider tweaking the establishment's tail. It went wrong for many reasons, many of them Laker's direct responsibility, coupled with some cruel bad luck when the world economy went universally sour at the wrong time for his airline. It is probably impossible now that Laker can ever come back as the head of a major airline. He was 60 years of age in the summer following the bankruptcy. And there has been lots of publicity about the part played by his weaknesses in the broader area of management. Even the job as the public figure-head of a recreated airline seems beyond him. And, in any case, he wouldn't like not being in charge.

He always said he would not like to be poor again. While Laker is far from being down to his last few pounds, he is the most obvious loser from the bankruptcy. His horse stud, farm, house, luxury yacht and his prized Rolls-Royce and Jaguar had 'For Sale' signs put on them. He was rapidly stripped of his membership at Lloyd's of London, the insurance underwriting centre of the world, whose members have to accept unlimited risk on the insurance taken on by the partners. Laker had been a silent member since 1954, when the entry fee was £75,000. He had to admit that 'bearing in mind Lloyd's continuing means test requirements', he had better cease underwriting. One of the greatest humiliations of all for status-conscious Laker must have been the airline industry's withdrawal of the free travel passes that are given to all airline presidents. It was these passes that had allowed Laker more or less unlimited access to fly Concorde across the Atlantic to New York or Washington. The airlines became embarrassed by the publicity that hit them when it became clear that Laker was travelling first-class for free when there were still Laker Airways' passengers who were stranded. The final blow was that Laker was obliged to put the Skytrain trade name on the market.

Most of the passengers who were stranded by Laker's Skytrain fared fairly well. While there was still good publicity to be garnered, other airlines carried home passengers with Laker return tickets. It was fortunate that the collapse took place at such a low point in world travel. Those that tried to get back a few weeks after the bankruptcy, when publicity had died down, found it harder. Passengers who had bought and paid for tickets but had yet to begin their travel fared worst, since they became unsecured creditors, who will have to take their chances with whatever the official receiver, Bill Mackey, can come up with.

The blows hit hard in less obvious places when there is a bankruptcy. Often the hardest hit are the small companies that provide local services: the people who supply clean towels, or sweep out the offices; the small firms that design and print brochures. They are not large enough to swallow such debts and shrug them off in the way that an oil company can with an unpaid fuel bill or the British Airport Authority with unpaid landing fees.

The largest sums involved concern the aircraft makers. McDonnell Douglas wrote off $48 million in 1981 to cover Laker's debts and General Electric $10 million. And British Aerospace made a provision of £8 million in its accounts for the year ended March 1981 to cover the first-loss guarantee on Laker's Airbuses. It seems likely, however, that in time these sums will be recovered. Laker looked after his equipment well and as it is sold or leased out, so the first-losses will be recovered.

The only obvious gainers from all this are the other airlines that had to compete with Laker. They all made pious statements about how sad the bankruptcy was, but their private thoughts showed otherwise. The boss of one continental airline, who barely knew Laker but who opposed absolutely his free-market ideas, said, after the collapse: 'The only big thing about Laker was his mouth.' That sums up the views of most of the established airlines. They prefer to compete their own way, within the cosy confines of their cartel, IATA.

The corollary of all this, of course, is that the losers in the long run will be the travelling public. Laker did not directly change much that wasn't already happening to international aviation, but he was a marvellous catalyst. His presence made those changes happen faster. His absence will see the market revert to its old, carved-up ways faster, too. More's the pity.